■■■
''WANNA BE MY FRIEND?''

"WANNA BE MY FRIEND?"

HOW TO STRENGTHEN YOUR CHILD'S SOCIAL SKILLS

Leanne Domash, Ph.D., with Judith Sachs

HEARST BOOKS
New York

Published by arrangement with
Skylight Press,
260 West 72nd Street, Suite 6-C,
New York , NY 10023

Library of Congress Cataloging-in-Pubication Data

Domash, Leanne.
     "Wanna be my friend?" : how to strengthen your child's social
skills / Leanne Domash with Judith Sachs.—1st ed.
          p.   cm.—(Good housekeeping parent guides)
     "A Skylight Press book."
     Includes bibliographical references and index.
     ISBN 0-688-11936-0
     1. Friendship in children.   2. Social skills in children.
3. Child rearing. I. Sachs, Judith, 1947–   II. Title.
III. Series.
BF723.F68D66   1994
302.3′4′083—dc20   93-11910
                                                              CIP

Printed in the United States of America

First Edition

1 2 3 4 5 6 7 8 9 10

BOOK DESIGN BY DANA KASARSKY DESIGN

ABOUT THE GOOD HOUSEKEEPING PARENT GUIDES

Children are a most wonderful gift in our lives—and they are also a challenge! That's why, nine years ago, we created *Good Housekeeping*'s largest-ever special editorial section: the Child Care section. Winner of a National Magazine Award in 1988, this annual section has grown by leaps and bounds to comprise more than one hundred pages, featuring articles from such notable collaborators as the American Academy of Pediatrics and the Bank Street College of Education.

THE GOOD HOUSEKEEPING PARENT GUIDES continue this spirit of helping parents meet the challenges of childrearing. Written by uniquely qualified authorities, these lively, informative books invite you to explore in depth the everyday challenges of parenting. They are filled with ideas, examples, and strategies drawn from the real-life situations we all encounter with children. They offer new ways to understand and respond to children, as well as guidance on handling our own needs as parents.

We hope you find these guides valuable additions to your home library, providing new insights into your children, as well as innovative ideas to consider in your role as a parent. Most of all, we hope that they contribute to the loving bond you share with your child.

—JOHN MACK CARTER
Editor-in-Chief
Good Housekeeping

ACKNOWLEDGMENTS

I want to thank Ken Theil for his love, devotion, and support, without which this book could not have been completed. Thanks also to dear colleagues and friends Dr. Lawrence Balter and Karen Adams for their recommendation, support, and good humor.

Many colleagues, friends, and relatives have been helpful and wise, but especially Drs. Joan Zuckerberg, Roy Shapiro, and Michael Varga, and my brother, Jack Goldstein, Esq., and my aunt and uncle, Alice and Ed Leimseider. Elaine and Herb Stevens of Westport, Massachusetts, dear friends, have provided counsel and great discussion in an inspirational setting in their home by the river.

I thank my writer, Judith Sachs, for her dedication and professionalism in translating my ideas into enjoyable prose. Thanks also to Toni Sciarra, our editor, for her thoughtful and incisive guidance and direction. Lastly, I thank Lynn Sonberg and Meg Schneider of Skylight Press for their creativity, insight, and hard work in making this dream come true.

CONTENTS

When two children meet for the first time on a playground, on a sand dune at the beach, or in a schoolroom, certain codes are passed and hidden messages are acknowledged as two thinking, feeling creatures join in a mutual desire to play:

> *"Let's move that rock."*
> *"Give me to fifteen, then you start running."*
> *"I'll take the long skirt; you wear the sequins."*

Directives are given in shorthand, but a great deal is happening beneath the surface. What is really going on is a mystery to most of us. As we stand back and observe, we may wonder how our kids actually feel during these seemingly simple social interactions. What we may fail to consider, however, is how these early relationships will affect them in later life.

Until now, children's friendship has been a silent aspect of growing up. Our own parents probably didn't pay much attention to our playmates until we were in our adolescent years and they worried about "bad influences" and "hanging out with the wrong crowd." Now we know that children's friendships throughout childhood are crucial to later intimacies. The way our sons and daughters learn to play, to share, to fight, to feel empathy, is vital to their later development as well-rounded social individuals with wide emotional range. The better our social skills as children, the more likely we are to grow into compassionate, socially intelligent adults with a strong sense of belonging and self-worth.

In addition, children today are exposed to social situations from the cradle: Parents introduce their kids in strollers at the park or send their children to day care or organize playgroups so that Johnny and Susie can learn—even before they can talk—what it means to get along with others. It's vital that we understand children's friendship behaviors, especially at these early ages, since what may appear unusual or downright barbaric to us may be perfectly normal in the scheme of children's healthy development. We owe it to our children to help them have the best experiences with friends they possibly can at every age.

There are scores of self-help and parenting books to improve relationships between mothers and daughters, mothers and sons, fathers and daughters, fathers and sons, and everyone all together. There are also useful books on dealing with sibling rivalry and grandparenting. But it's time to acknowledge that some of the most basic relationships happen *outside* the home environment. Childhood friendships give a kid new chances to build self-esteem. They may even offer the opportunity to make up for the understanding or guidance that a child may lack at home. A good friend can teach your child about give-and-take, about loss and gain, and your child can learn to respond in kind. The tight friendships children form may correct a lot of the miscommunications that can occur even in the best of family settings.

This book will help you to understand your child's

friendships and to encourage your child's capacity for dealing with others. Just as we all have verbal and mathematical skills, or musical or athletic ability, we also have the potential for honing our social skills. We can learn to lead *and* follow; we can practice confiding *and* listening; we can be part of a best-friend couple or stand away and reflect on that best friend with another friend.

We don't come into the world having mastered those gargantuan tasks, however. At first our children will have to struggle just to move one rock with a little cooperation; to wait the appropriate amount of time before they start the race; to relinquish the flashy sequins and wear the plain long skirt so that their friend will like them and want to play with them again.

Some children have more trouble getting the hang of friendship than others, and parents can do a great deal for kids who seem to have trouble in social settings. Those who are difficult to reach because they are enormously sensitive or overly aggressive can be helped. They can learn to modify their behavior and bring out the best in themselves as individuals and as pals. This book offers a way to work with kids who need an extra bridge to better friendships.

The philosopher William James said, "Wherever you are, it is your own friends who make your world." John Lennon concurred: "I get by with a little help from my friends."

What can be more important than giving our children their birthright—the opportunities to bond with others, strangers at first glance and then, with time, those in whom we trust and for whom we feel the deepest human emotion? This book will point the way toward the rich possibilities that your child will reap from being with good friends.

—LEANNE DOMASH, PH.D.
New York, 1994

■■

''WANNA BE MY FRIEND?''

1

THE CRITICAL VALUE OF FRIENDSHIP

Sometimes you need a friend. Someone to talk to, to trust, to care about, to laugh with.

Friends can be the lifeblood of our emotional existence. They are as vital for our kids as they are for us, because childhood friendships—their tone, their intensity, and their emotional content—reverberate loudly in adult relationships.

Many in the last generation relied on family above all— you were born into a circle of people who were supposed to "be there" for you whether they liked you or not. And you were supposed to do the same for them. However, today in a society where neither the traditional nuclear family nor the extended family is standard anymore, we and our children must often rely on other human bonds for continuity, security, and understanding.

A good friend can give a child an honest window into his own soul, a reflection of the way he sees the world and how it sees him. And the bonds our children forge in their earliest years allow them to explore relationships more freely and successfully later on.

Did you know that . . .

- Childhood friendships are the best training ground for intimacy and stable marriages
- Children who have trouble making and keeping friends are more likely to fail in school and may be at greater risk for divorce in later life
- Teenagers who can't make or keep friends, because they're either loners or bullies, are more likely to commit suicide
- Children can get the affection, support, and security they're missing in an unhappy home from a good friend
- Children develop values and ethics through the give-and-take of close friendships
- Warm, giving parents don't always raise warm children who can easily connect with others
- A parent who interferes in a heated argument between three-year-olds may be robbing his or her child of a chance to learn to handle feelings
- Parents who don't set limits on their children's behavior may be making it difficult for them to develop close friendships—or any friendships at all
- Children who know how to make and keep friends tend not to become depressed
- Interfering with your child's choice of friends—no matter how bad they seem to you—is at times the worst thing you can do.

Childhood friendships form a training ground for life.

PARENTS' CONCERNS ABOUT
THEIR CHILDREN'S FRIENDSHIPS

All parents worry about their children's friendships: "Is my child popular? Why does she have only one friend? Why is he so bossy with the other kids? Does she give in too much? Why do the other kids gang up on my son? Why are my daughter and her friend so preoccupied with bodily functions? Why does my child talk to her best friend about subjects she should be discussing with me? Why does my son insist on playing with that obnoxious boy down the block—won't he pick up that boy's bad habits?"

It's often hard to distance ourselves from what we *assume* our child is feeling, perhaps because every one of us carries some painful scars from our own early friendships. Memories of rejection, loneliness, and confusion linger, and we would do anything to spare our children those heartbreaking moments we remember all too well.

But we can't protect our kids from life—nor should we. Learning to be a friend and to accept others' friendship is a long process of hard-won lessons. A child can't learn it in school or from her parents. She becomes a good friend by *practicing friendship:* by connecting with other boys, girls, and adults; by developing social skills that "click" with others.

Our children will develop into good friends by honing their strengths and making their own mistakes. They will develop friendships that complement their temperaments— sometimes linking up with someone whose personality is the opposite of theirs, but sometimes finding it more comfortable to be with someone just as outgoing or just as shy as they are. Sometimes they learn what they need to know about friendship by picking the wrong friend.

As parents it's not our job to choose our children's friends the way we choose their names or where they go to school. Instead we need to give them the latitude to make their own choices, even if these turn out to be difficult ones. We need to give them the room to make errors, to guide them when they ask us to, and to comfort them when things don't work out.

Our role in this process cannot be overestimated. We must remain objective and care deeply; suggest ways of coping, but never dominate. This kind of participation in our child's life is much more subtle, and much more difficult, than any other type of parenting we may do.

NEW RESEARCH FINDINGS

As compelling new research in child development has shown, children have different types of intelligence that blossom with the right encouragement. According to Dr. Howard Gardner, whose 1985 book, *Frames of Mind,* outlined the different forms of intelligence, interpersonal intelligence is of tremendous importance in life. Gardner points out that being smart is not simply a matter of I.Q. Some of the most successful individuals are those who know how to use their social "smarts" to improve themselves and their relationships with others, and to get ahead, regardless of how well or badly they score on tests or how many languages they know or whether or not they can design a building. Parents can help their child to develop a finely tuned social intelligence when they know what to do about different friendship issues.

Whereas in the past, psychologists and psychiatrists believed that the family dynamic was the chief modeling influence on children's emotional well-being and self-esteem, research has proven that *early friendships have a very powerful effect on children's sense of self and their development into assured, confident adults.* Many doctors now posit that the lack of such bonds can pose lifelong health risks.

One eminent professor of education and psychiatry at

Harvard University, Dr. Robert L. Selman, believes that early friendship is a crucial factor in our ability to establish intimate relationships. Selman and his associate, Dr. Lynn H. Schultz, are two pioneers in the child-development field who credit later interpersonal successes or failures in life to the influences of childhood friendships. Selman's innovative work showed that a child's ability to consider someone else's perspective is an indicator of maturity and competence in later relationships.

Dr. Thomas Hatch, also from Harvard University, has isolated four primary social skills that help children both in and out of group situations: Some kids are leaders, some can mediate arguments, some can empathize well with their friends, and some excel at analyzing social interactions.

Dr. William Damon synthesized others' work on a child's developmental progression in friendship skills, and Dr. Kenneth Dodge at Duke University explained how children use these skills expertly, pretty well, or weakly, allowing us to credit them with high, medium, or low social intelligence.

Other seminal studies in this field were done by Dr. Stella Chess and Dr. Alexander Thomas, whose groundbreaking work on children's patterns of temperament parallels our discussion of social styles in Chapter Two. According to Chess and Thomas, each of us is born with certain ingrained personality traits that greatly affect our ability to relate to others.

To all of these researchers, and to others at Vanderbilt University, the University of Washington, and Pennsylvania State, I owe an enormous debt. My own findings concur with their fascinating evidence that the child who can trust and love a friend is going to be an adult with valuable and sophisticated interpersonal skills—someone who is able to solve problems in the workplace as well as maintain a variety of close love relationships.

FRIENDSHIP—THE THIRD BIG CHANCE
IN OUR EMOTIONAL LIFE

The first bond we develop is the one we form with the person who brought us into the world. A mother is emotionally there for her infant most of his waking or sleeping life.

Then, around the age of two or three, we begin to work on our next big relationship—the one we develop (or don't develop) with our fathers. True closeness with our father, experts say, can help us begin to separate from the bond with the mother, and move "out into the world." It can also, if necessary, make up for the lacks in that relationship.

Then comes our third big chance in life. As we continue to become more independent, we expand on these two experiences by testing our capacity for closeness on our friends. Interestingly, friends may often be better than siblings at helping us develop as individuals, since sibling relationships are often complicated by age differences and competition for parents' attention.

We can learn things from our friends that we simply can't "get" within the family structure. Parents can discipline us and can decree what's fair and what's not, but how do we really get the message until we try it out on a friend? This third chance at intimacy is the laboratory where we test what we've learned within the family.

Children teach each other right and wrong by making decisions together about what to do or how to act. It's not enough to know that another person wants something from you—you must also begin to *feel* how someone else feels. In developing this capacity to combine knowledge with emotion, a child figures out how to "do the right thing." He doesn't just *know* what's fair, he actually *comprehends* the ethics of right and wrong because he feels the consequences of his actions deep inside.

A LOOK AT THREE FRIENDSHIPS

We hear their giggles and see their happy faces as they play together. We're witnesses to their angry outbursts and referees for their battles. But do we really understand what's going on in our children's social lives?

These parents don't:

Three-year-old Andrew was a pincher. Whenever he was angry or upset, he singled out one boy in his playgroup and would pinch him hard enough to produce screams of agony. Andrew's mother was mortified by his behavior, which was just the opposite of his normally sweet disposition. She wondered if he acted this way because of something she was doing—or not doing—and worried that the other parents secretly blamed her for her son's aggressiveness. Whenever Andrew pinched another boy, she would warn him sharply about punishment, but none of her threats did any good. Finally she and Andrew left the playgroup.

* * *

Mark's mother had mixed feelings about her five-year-old son's close friendship with Jessica, their neighbor's five-year-old. They were "best friends," Mark said. But he was strangely reticent about the game they often played, giggling behind the closed bathroom door. One day, determined to get to the bottom of the mystery, Mark's mother knocked on the bathroom door and swung it open. There were Mark and Jessica sitting naked on the floor, playing house with bathtub toys that represented their imaginary family.

Mark's mother panicked. "Mark, get your clothes back on!" she shrieked. "Nice boys and girls don't do that!" She threw the kids' shorts and shirts at them and hustled them out of the room. She was certain she had just seen her worst fears realized—that Mark and Jessica were oversexed. "I never want to see the two of you alone in here again!" she scolded.

* * *

Jennifer's mother came home from work one evening, exhausted and depressed over an argument she and her husband had had that morning. It was just one more in an escalating series of disputes she and her husband had been having. Walking past Jennifer's room, she overheard her eight-year-old daughter giving her best friend, Betsy, a blow-by-blow description of the fight. Betsy's sympathetic response (which included the phrase "dumb grown-ups") horrified Jennifer's mother. She stalked into Jennifer's room and confronted her. "What goes on in this family is private," she told her daughter with barely controlled rage. "I'm sure you and Betsy can find other things to talk about than our personal business." She walked out, only dimly aware of the stricken look on Jennifer's face.

BEHIND THE CLOSED DOORS
OF CHILDREN'S FRIENDSHIPS

For many adults, as these three case histories illustrate, children's lives are as mysterious as the cultures we might find on distant planets. We know neither the customs nor the language. Without understanding exactly how children develop, and what their changing needs are, we view our children's inner lives from our own perspectives. But these are dramatically different! Often much of what is going on we *can't* see. And what we *think* we see may not be going on at all.

Take Andrew's mother, for example. She's afraid her three-year-old is becoming a bully. She knows he's taking out his frustrations in an inappropriate way. But at age three *he* doesn't know that. By striking out at his playmates, he's acting in a way that makes perfect sense to him. During this developmental stage children live in an egocentric world and are usually unable to see any point of view but their own. Andrew doesn't realize that his pinching hurts his friend, nor does he particularly care. A three-year-old protects his own interests by being purely physical.

Mark's mother's attitude shows that abnormality, like beauty, is in the eye of the beholder. She was uninformed and unnecessarily anxious about what the two children were doing. Mark is in no more danger of becoming a "sex maniac" than he is of sprouting wings. In fact Mark's behavior is perfectly normal and healthy. Many children between the ages of five and seven are aware of their sexuality. Mark and Jessica weren't engaging in sex play but in *sex-role* play, undressing and playacting at being parents in order to practice the part. In a few years Mark is likely to think of getting undressed with a friend as "yucky" and won't want to be reminded of the bathroom incident. By the time he's seven or eight, like most children, he'll enter a period where sex will be of minor interest. This period usually continues until adolescence, when he's ready to emerge, like a butterfly from its cocoon, as an independent person with a wide variety of interests, including sex.

Jennifer's mother let her own embarrassment and jealousy get in the way of Jennifer's need to confide in her friend. Because she felt her daughter should have turned to *her* as a confidante, she couldn't see that Jennifer has developed the beginning of an "adult" friendship. The capacity for greater intimacy becomes possible only when a child reaches the age of eight or nine. Jennifer turned to Betsy because she needed to talk to someone who was at once sympathetic and objective (qualities her mother lacks in this instance). She has truly "bonded" with another person, investing her trust and loyalty in Betsy so that she can share her most intimate and hurtful secrets. She knows she'll receive an empathetic response from this friend. And her newfound capacity for this more mature friendship will also help Jennifer weather the turbulent times in her parents' marriage.

WHICH IS THE RIGHT COURSE TO TAKE?

As these three parents' dilemmas illustrate, responding to our children's friendships is a complex and sensitive matter. It's tremendously important to know when to step in, when to step away, and when simply to observe and comfort. For many of us our first instinct may be to step in, because we can't bear to see our child in pain—most of us can remember that kind of pain all too well from our own childhood.

Or we might think we should step away, because we know it's important to foster independence (or maybe because our own parents never came to our rescue in a similar situation).

But there is a way to know how and when to become involved. Let's look at what these parents could have done differently had they been aware of what was really going on in their children's lives.

Andrew's mother, first by stepping in and then by pulling him away from the group, is denying him the opportunity to learn some new ways of dealing with frustration. Instead of shouting at him, she might have encouraged him to express his anger verbally. And if the other kids started excluding him from their play, he might learn on his own that pinching doesn't work. To get back in the group's good graces, he would have been forced to learn different ways of coping. His mother and father will have to understand that as he becomes more fluent in verbal anger, he may start bringing home his newfound skills, screaming at his parents when he's upset with them. Instead of punishing him for this, they'll have to acknowledge the improvement in his behavior: He isn't pinching or hitting, and he's letting out his feelings in an appropriate way.

Mark's mother jumped to a wrong conclusion, causing Mark to feel bad about himself, his body, and his good relationship with Jessica. She also made too much of their game. Instead of panicking, she could have taken a deep breath and suggested that they all go downstairs and play a game or bake cookies, calmly ending the private, secret moment that might have overstimulated the children.

Jennifer would like her mother to understand why she would confide in a trusted friend about this particular subject. Clearly her mother couldn't be objective about her marital problems, and Jennifer couldn't talk freely with her about them. By criticizing her daughter for this breach of family confidence, Mrs. Lewis damaged Jennifer's sense of self-worth and her comfort with the decision she'd made to talk to Betsy. Kids look to their parents for approval, and when they don't get it, they may feel depressed.

It's also possible that Jennifer's mother feels left out of her daughter's emotional life—at a time when *she* really needs someone. She would do a lot better to follow Jennifer's example and find a friend of her own to confide in. Then she could walk past Jennifer's room, having overheard her conversation with Betsy, and be grateful that her daughter felt secure enough with her pal to reach out for much-needed support. She might also feel proud that Jennifer has accomplished a developmental feat: Instead of blaming herself for her parents' marital problems (as many children do in a family crisis), Jennifer is allying herself with a companion who can help her.

Of course while too much interference in a child's friendships can wear away dangerously at a child's self-esteem, too little can also be harmful. One parent, recalling how her own parents had interfered in her relationships when she was little, did nothing when she heard her four-year-old call his friend stupid, and saw the other child rush from their yard in tears. What she might have done was take her son aside privately and explain how words can hurt people. This way she wouldn't be humiliating him in front of his friend, and she could later help him identify an opportunity to make up.

HOW PARENTS CAN FOSTER
GOOD FRIENDSHIP SKILLS

These three case histories point up a basic truth: It's important to take your children's friendships seriously. Remember, all of your child's friendships have critical value *to him.* Relax, though, even when you see glitches in your child's social growth. Just like walking, talking, and feeding oneself, friendship cannot be learned overnight. Children are always straddling developmental stages, and growth isn't a neat progression. Your child may take two steps forward and one back socially for a long time.

Children also act differently with different children. They may appear mature and calm with one friend and ridiculously silly with another. The idea is to let them experiment with many types of friends in many different settings so that they can experience the widest range of social contact.

There are many other things you can do to encourage your child's early relationships. The first step for any parent is to identify your child's social style. Is your child an extrovert who thrives in groups, no matter how large and raucous? Or is she an introvert who shies away from confrontation and would rather sit on the sidelines with a book than introduce herself to a potential new friend?

Of course there are extroverts who love to spend quiet time with a pet and introverts who somehow manage to shine when they can be coaxed to get up on a stage. But there are some specific social styles we'll point out to you, and one of these will fit your child. These styles correlate with different social skills. When you read the case histories in each chapter, you'll be able to see exactly what children of different social styles are like and what their social potential may be at a later development stage and in adulthood. You'll also be able to see how detrimental it can be to push them toward behaviors that are absolutely alien to them.

Once you know your child's social strengths and weaknesses, you can better gauge how he'll handle a tough situation and how you can prepare him for certain challenging events. You'll also know something about his untapped personal resources and will be able to identify the areas you need to help him work on for the future.

It's helpful as well to reach back into your own past and think about how you handled friendships. Maybe you were a loner and feel some residual pain when watching your own child's struggle to communicate with people. The temptation to try to push him along may sometimes be overwhelming. But when you can acknowledge that you and your child have different orientations toward social interactions, you can be less emotionally involved in the outcome.

You need to know, also, what kind of parent you are, because your style and your partner's have enormous ramifications on the way your child approaches others. A rule-oriented parent will set limits and show love and concern in a manner that is different from a laid-back parent. And the blend in your particular family will have an impact on your child's relationships with you and anyone else he deals with.

Once you have this background, in subsequent chapters you'll follow your child up the developmental ladder as you learn about parallel play, separation anxiety, negotiation strategies, sharing possessions, sexuality, empathy, altruism, selecting a best friend, taking another person's perspective, choosing between family and friends, opposite-sex intimacy, and peer pressure. Finally, you will learn about children who have more trouble than most reaching out socially, and what you can do for a child who tends to withdraw, become depressed, act out, or bully others.

In order to help you and your child through the intricacies of social interaction, we have designed specialized play kits for use with children of different ages. The kits, consisting of materials and exercises, can help you enhance your child's social intelligence and short-circuit problems that may arise. These kits offer ways to make your child feel comfortable and familiar with all types of relationship issues.

The Social Skills Play Kit, in Chapter Four, offers a list of materials and exercises that will allow you to explore friendship skills with children ages eighteen months to six or seven years. The Social Skills Verbal Kit, in Chapter Seven, is designed for use with children from ages seven or eight to twelve and takes a more sophisticated approach to playacting around friendship issues. Two other exercise sections, "Developing Your Child's Empathy" and "Looking in From the Other Side: Taking Mutual Perspectives" are found in chapters Six and Eight respectively. These two sets of verbal games will allow you and your child to explore the new feelings that arise in children's friendships as they become more mature.

By using the exercises and play kits, you will gain the skills you need to foster the best friendship skills in your child and to act as a champion for your child's successes and a buffer for his difficulties.

If you can pay attention to what's going on for your child socially, without judging, forbidding, or pushing, you will be providing him with countless opportunities to become a strong link in the chain of individuals that make up our world.

2

SOCIAL SKILLS, SOCIAL STYLES

Eavesdrop at any playground or PTA meeting—anywhere parents gather—and you will hear something like this:

"My Alex just doesn't stick up for himself. He'll do anything another kid dares him to do!"

"Jane is such a show-off. I wish she'd give the other kids a chance on the slide."

"I'd really like my kid to join the team, but he takes everything so personally, he'd cry if the coach said boo to him."

"I've got the class clown—no matter what's going on, he gets people to laugh by acting silly."

"I guess there must be something the matter with mine—she's so easygoing and adaptable!"

Parents—talking about their children. But notice that they aren't describing their kids per se. They are placing their child in a social setting and talking about the ways that he or she fits in or doesn't. They are referring to the *social skills* necessary for anyone to make his or her way in the world.

These parents are pointing out that their child uses his skills in a certain way, based on his own attitudes and qualities. These qualities represent your child's unique *social style* of behavior, which has probably been with him, in various stages of development, since birth. You know when you have a typically moody kid; a shy one; a child who's happy, worried, adaptable, and so on. Although no one reacts the same way on every occasion—we are able to adapt our behavior to the situation—there certainly is enough consistency in our responses to say that social style influences everything we do and say.

As we become more experienced in life, our social style and skills become more sophisticated and complex. This on-going process creates our *social intelligence*. A high social intelligence for a child is an excellent foundation for later intimacy with members of both sexes and provides a good set of tools for working with others at play, school, business, and home.

In this chapter we'll talk about social skills and social style and discuss how they change as your child grows and his social intelligence develops.

HOW DO WE "GET SMART" SOCIALLY?

Some of us are good at math, some at verbal skills. Some of us can look at a complicated set of physical movements and repeat them perfectly in sequence and with the right rhythm. Some of us can hear a tune played on the piano and hum it right back, with crescendos and decrescendos in all the right places.

And some of us always seem to know how to act in any social situation. The concept of *social intelligence* is the ability to function effectively with one or two other people or in a group. The best time to develop our skills for social "smarts" is when we're very young.

It's essential that our social intelligence mesh with all our other abilities as we grow to adulthood. For example, it's not enough to be a brilliant English teacher who knows literature and writing unless you have the social intelligence to exchange your ideas fruitfully with others in an academic setting. It's not enough to be a crackerjack marketing executive who knows statistics and data bases inside out unless you have a high enough social intelligence to work with people on the job.

We can see how social intelligence works by looking at two different children in a playground, standing outside a group, wanting to join it. One seven-year-old, Samantha, sees that the others have found something on the ground and are gathered around it. She hears one child say, "Yuck! What is that?" and uses this verbal cue to go over and see if she can identify the object of their fascination.

"It's not a beetle, is it?" she asks, leaving the door open for an answer from somebody else. Effortlessly she moves close to the child who has bent down to examine the bug, physically putting herself close to the one who appears to be the leader.

"Ugh. Who'd want to touch that?" another child says.

"Scaredy-cat," taunts a third.

Samantha connects with both kids now and stops the potential conflict between them by scooping up the dead bug herself. "This kind isn't poisonous. My brother showed me a picture in a book last night. But it's a good idea not to touch them unless you know they're safe. I used to be so afraid of these things," she says. "Now I just think they're kind of gross."

Samantha has the ability to size up how a group functions and how she fits into it. She didn't rush the other kids, but joined them when the time seemed right to her, on their turf, in order to solve their problem. She made peace by taking some initiative without being pushy (picking up the bug and accommodating the kid who was scared). Samantha has real rapport with others.

Now let's look at what Katie, also seven, does in the same situation. She approaches the children and says, "Hey, what are you all doing over here staring at that ugly bug? I'm going to play on the swings."

When no one joins her, she hugs the outskirts of the group, trying to get someone's attention. "I can hit the top of those branches when I swing," she brags to one of the kids. When they keep talking about the bug, she finally comes over and shoves it with her foot.

"Hey, what are you doing?" one boy demands.

"I hate it; it's gross," Katie complains.

"Don't squash it," he yells at her. "I want it for my collection."

Katie turns on her heel and stomps away. "I'm going to the swings," she declares.

Katie couldn't really join in because she didn't appreciate what the kids were interested in, she didn't wait a sufficient period of time for them to change their focus to what she was doing, and she got into a conflict, then walked away from it. Her social intelligence is not nearly as high as Samantha's, and the skills she needs to negotiate entering a group aren't well developed.

We'll see what skills are needed for high social intelligence later in this chapter. Right now, let's look at the steps the two girls took that made the group include or exclude them:

1. **Standing back.** A successful strategy for a child entering a group that's already formed is to do some strategic hovering. You'll note that Samantha just stood and watched first. By doing this she got a feeling for the group as a whole, not just one or two children in the group. She made comments to the children about what they were doing and then

waited for a response. This way she was able to put herself in the other kids' places. She could feel *empathy* for all of them—that is, the ability to feel as they feel in a particular situation. By seeing how the other children reacted to her, listening to their words, and observing their body language, Samantha knew the right time to make her move to connect with the others and join the group.

2. **Connecting.** Once she'd sized up the situation, Samantha asked *without words* if she could join their game: She moved closer, physically readying herself to enter the group. This nonverbal rapport was essential before she could make the next move.

3. **Joining In.** Once Samantha was in the game, she assessed her position. Was she a leader or a follower? Did the others listen to her or make fun of her? How did she take it? Unlike Katie, who left the group before really joining it, Samantha sensed when to be assertive and when to hold back for a while, based on the way the other kids received her.

Everything involved in social intelligence perpetuates the life of a group. A child who keeps a play session going by starting an activity and getting kids to follow the rules is socially intelligent. If she also has empathy for those who are having troubles and can help them get along with others in the group, that's socially intelligent. If she can negotiate a conflict to its ultimate solution—maybe even find several possible solutions that will appeal to different members of the group—that's *extremely* socially intelligent.

Some children move easily toward this intelligence, but most kids need gentle steering in the right direction. Remember that emotional growth and development is not linear: Two steps forward toward helping a younger friend learn to ride a bike may be followed by one backward—when the "helper" dares the younger child to race him on that bike or else be branded a sissy. This is perfectly normal and is to be expected. In addition, remember that your child is playing with other kids who are at different social stages themselves. So don't be surprised when your child vacillates between being babyish and mature, kind and cruel. It's the mix of these behaviors that make children's friendships so unpredictably wonderful, miserable, volatile, and edifying.

USING SOCIAL SKILLS
TO FORGE FRIENDSHIPS

What are the basic skills we need to be able to move through life, mixing and matching our social styles with those of others?

Thomas C. Hatch, Ph.D, a child-development specialist at Harvard University, describes four different approaches to being socially skillful. In a paper entitled "Social Intelligence in Young Children," delivered at a meeting of the American Psychological Association, Boston, Massachusetts, August 1990, he describes children as either "leaders," who organize groups; "mediators," who negotiate conflicts; "empathizers," who know how to connect to others; and "therapists," who are good analyzers of social situations.

We can break these skills down even more finely. To some extent all of us have the eight essential social abilities listed below, but depending on our social styles, we excel in some and are weaker in others:

- Leadership/charisma
- Nonverbal rapport/sense of timing
- Peacemaking skills
- Empathy
- Ability to wait and observe
- Willingness and ability to join in
- Ability to follow rules
- Sense of enthusiasm and fun

Once you understand what these essential skills are, you must understand just how they manifest themselves in your child. A charismatic child who is a natural leader, for example, will have a very different mode of settling a dispute between two other friends than an empathic child would. The former would be more directive and authoritative with her friends. The latter would try to understand all sides of the argument before attempting to reach a conciliation.

We're going to help you figure out the kind of child you have, which, as you'll see, is probably a blend of two or three social styles. Then we'll identify the strengths and weaknesses of those styles. This way you'll be able to recognize your child's natural building blocks of social intelligence.

WHAT IS YOUR CHILD'S SOCIAL STYLE?

When I ask parents what their child is like, most of them refuse to be pinned down. They'll say, "My child is a little bit of everything—a sports fanatic, a thinker, kind to others, demanding when he needs to get his own way, generally happy, often worried, and so on." Nobody wants to pigeon-hole the fantastic, small individuals we've brought into the world, who make our lives so infinitely interesting and always surprising.

But you can probably zero in on two or three salient features that are *always* present in your child. There's generally one basic style she conforms to, another she may rely on in times of stress, and perhaps even a blend of those two plus a third that help to create the complex individual she is.

Some of the most important research on children's temperament was done by Dr. Stella Chess and Dr. Alexander Thomas, two prominent child-development specialists. These psychiatrists subscribe to the belief, as I do, that an important part of our personality is biologically based. Some babies enter life screaming for attention; others are mild-mannered and so polite, they hardly squeak even when wet or hungry. Chess and Thomas define children as either easy, difficult, or slow to warm up. These inborn qualities develop as our children develop and are shaped by outside forces—parental guidance being the first and foremost.

A person is never just one type, but becomes, over time and space and influence, a blend of types. So a colicky, fussy baby may grow up to be a demanding person, but one with a special ability to understand others' problems and help resolve them.

Through my years of working with parents and children, I've expanded the idea of temperament and types into a larger framework. The inherent characteristics that make up each individual reveal themselves in ten different social styles, each of which has many blends. We use our special style within all the various relationships we develop in life.

As you examine the ten styles I've identified below, you will surely find your child (and yourself!):

• **The Boss:** This child is a leader, but may go overboard in his desire to get others to move his way. He is usually enthusiastic and upbeat, because he's confident about knowing how he wants things to go. He may tend to be controlling and push others around, and needs to be made more aware of others' feelings.

• **The Follower:** He hasn't quite found his sense of self yet, so it's easily shaken by anyone with a stronger personality. This can make him very likable, but sometimes, he is popular at the expense of being true to himself. For this reason it's important to encourage him to define his own likes and dislikes and firm up his opinions.

• **The Performer:** This child loves to be center-stage. He can be dramatic and lots of fun to be with. It's important to encourage his interest in others' abilities so that he doesn't feel he's the only one to be admired and seen.

- **The Thinker:** She has excellent inner resources and enjoys being alone. Though she's not propelled toward social activities, she can function well on the outskirts of a group, using her mind to work things out. She may have few friends and may need help reaching out and connecting to others.
- **The Team Player:** She is a leader, a popular kid, well coordinated emotionally and physically. She relies on her physical talents to make her way effectively through the world.
- **The Shy Child:** She is a thoughtful and understanding person, but needs help plunging into any group. She just has to do it at her own pace. Being pushed to perform or answer a question or meet a new child can be truly painful for her. She will find transitions between events easier to master if she's prepared for them in advance.
- **The Strong-Willed Child:** This child is usually outgoing and playful and is sure of her own opinions and desires. Unlike the Boss, she doesn't need to persuade others to do what she wants, so long as she can assert her own ideas. While the Boss is a controlling leader, the Strong-Willed Child is more self-contained—her basic need is to get what she wants for herself. She can be ambitious, persevering, and goal-oriented. But if she's anxious that things may not go her way, she may lack flexibility and become a persistent nag.
- **The Fragile Flower:** She can relate to others and have fun, but she tends to "take things" wrong. She backs away from conflict because she doesn't think highly enough of her own opinion to defend it against an attacker. Unlike the Follower, who is comfortable as long as someone else is leading, the Fragile Flower is always looking over her shoulder, thinking that others may be criticizing her. This is a child who needs lots of support to be able to come forward in a group and not feel so easily hurt.
- **The Naysayer:** This child is very self-protective, saying no to any suggestion just to make sure he isn't going to

get himself into a situation he doesn't like. This is a child who needs a lot of preparation for any change of activity or mood, and it's helpful to give him a feeling that he can make choices—within prescribed limits of course. If you can convince this child to examine his alternatives more thoughtfully, he'll learn how to make good decisions and choices on his own as he gets older.

• **The Adapter:** This is the "go with the flow" kid. His naturally easy rhythms allow him to adjust to almost any situation immediately. He can usually maintain his sense of self in a group, but if he's too adaptable, he may need help sorting out his own needs and speaking up for what he wants.

As we know, there is no way to codify the elusive changes of character and mood in our kids. Sometimes your daughter may sulk and refuse to do anything, while at other times she may be so exuberant about life, she seems to burst from one activity to the next. This indicates that like most healthy, normal people, she is flexible and can blend many of the qualities on our list. In trying to figure out your child's basic style, remember that we all have certain constellations of character traits that define us—and these are the ones we're attempting to identify.

MATCHING SOCIAL SKILLS AND SOCIAL STYLES

The chart on page 44 matches social skills with social styles. The circles on the grid tell you which social skills your child probably has already, based on his dominant social style. He currently relies on those skills in many of his interactions with others. However, the grid also indicates which social skills are beneath the surface in your child, waiting to be nurtured. These are represented on the chart by squares. Having identified these potential skills, you can encourage them when situations present themselves.

Finally, the grid shows you what you already know—the qualities that do not come naturally to your child. These are represented on the chart by triangles. If you attempt to steer him toward these behaviors, you may get no reaction, or a negative reaction. But over time, as your child realizes what his strengths and lacks are, he will be better able to maneuver successfully in social situations.

You may have noticed that your child may exhibit her most positive traits when she's feeling at ease and self-confident, but that her weaknesses become more evident when she's tired or under stress. Your daughter might be a Strong-Willed girl most of the time, and become a Naysayer at the end of a long day, or when she's thrust into a new situation over which she feels she has no control.

RESPECTING YOUR CHILD'S SOCIAL STYLE

As a parent it's your job to be aware of the changes in your child and help her use the social skills she naturally has even when she's not feeling her best or when a situation is particularly challenging. For example, by pointing out to a shy child how she occasionally rises to a social occasion, you can help her to stand in the spotlight every once in a while. You can teach a strong-willed child patience and reward him for deferring some of his needs to a later time.

And you can learn not to demand more than your child is currently capable of. Age is an important variable. It would be unfair to expect your two-year-old to have the savvy in a group that your seven-year-old possesses.

Your child may develop some of her skills later than those in her age group, and be precocious in developing others. If you try to push your child's basic style in a direction

SOCIAL SKILLS

Social Type	Leadership Charisma	Nonverbal Rapport/ Sense of Timing	Finding Solutions/ Making Peace	Empathy and Consideration	Wait/ Observe/ Analyze Situations	Willing-ness/ Ability to Participate	Follow Rules/ Maintain Group Activities	Sense of Enthusiasm and Fun
Boss	○	○	△	△	□	□	△	□
Follower	△	△	□	□	□	○	○	□
Performer	○	○	□	△	△	○	□	○
Thinker	△	□	○	□	○	□	□	□
Team Player	○	○	○	□	□	○	○	○
Shy Child	△	□	□	○	○	△	□	□
Strong-Willed Child	□	△	□	△	□	□	△	○
Fragile Flower	△	△	□	□	□	△	□	□
Naysayer	□	△	△	△	□	□	△	□
Adapter	□	○	○	○	□	○	○	○

○ Child usually has this trait
   Positive strength of this child

□ Child usually has good potential to develop this

△ Usually not a strength—use tact to develop

it cannot logically go, you may bring on some serious problems. First, you will be telling your child you don't approve of her the way she is, and this may seriously undermine her self-esteem. Second, you will be asking her to put a false facade on her genuine style, and her real self may get buried, which could make her feel isolated and depressed. Then, too, you may get nowhere—it's very hard to make anyone become something other than what she was born to be.

If you foster the strengths in your child's repertoire, you will see that the weaknesses tend to correct themselves or become less problematic. The child who has confidence in his effectiveness is better able to cope with his limitations.

HOW CHILDREN GROW INTO
THEIR NATURAL BLENDS

Our children aren't one shade or another. They are an entire rainbow of hues, shifting daily, hourly, even sometimes in microseconds, depending on mood, environment, other kids, and dozens of other outside influences.

"My daughter Peggy is incredibly sensitive and shy," one mother of a first-grader said. "Last year in kindergarten she had this awful teacher who pressured her and yelled at her for the slightest little thing. She had to stand up on a stage with sixty other kids in a school play, and she was totally miserable, sobbing the entire time. I felt her pain and wanted to rescue her so badly! But I thought, well, this is the real world, honey, and sometimes you have to do things you hate.

"This year there was a Christmas pageant. I was all set to beg Peggy's first-grade teacher—who's a wonderful, compassionate woman—to let Peggy do costumes or props or something. But then Peggy started coming home from school talking about the rehearsals, saying that she thought that maybe she could get through the play. After a few days of complaints about standing up too long and having too many lines to learn, she started bragging a little about her part. She sang me the song she was going to perform with three other children and explained how she had helped teach it to one little girl who was having trouble learning it.

"Next she got nervous about her costume—she wasn't sure she wanted to wear one for fear she'd 'look silly.' But when she found out it was purple—her favorite color—suddenly she was ecstatic about it. And the night of the performance I sat there in the auditorium with tears running down my cheeks, watching my formerly Nervous Nellie singing and dancing onstage in front of two hundred parents! I thought, 'Is this really my child!?' "

Yes, it certainly is her child! It is her child one year older, with a deeper ability to analyze a "dangerous" situation before fleeing from it and with a sensitive teacher who was able to help her shine.

If we look at Peggy in relation to our chart, we will see that she has grown into a blend of the Shy Child and the Adapter (last year, under lots of stress, she was more of a Fragile Flower). She still holds back in many ways, but she can now size up a situation more clearly. Her own understanding of what it's like to feel afraid makes her considerate of others' fears. Without the stress of the overbearing teacher, she's more active in finding solutions to potential problems.

Peggy has accomplished a great deal in a short period of time. Probably in the future she'll still need help developing leadership and negotiating skills and picking up on others' nonverbal cues, which are subtler than the deliberate, verbal instruction she takes so well.

It's a good idea to keep a Social Skills and Styles chart for your child, starting at a very early age, updating it every year or so. You will be delighted to see how time can heal many behavior problems and mold a happy, socially intelligent child.

DIFFERENT PATHS TO SOCIAL SKILLS

Let's see how two different extroverted children might turn out to be leaders. A Boss's keen awareness of others' weaknesses will tell him precisely the right moment to move to a stronger position. He's like a good pitcher, sensing just the right time to throw the curve ball when the batter's expecting a fastball.

A Strong-Willed Child can also be a leader, but he won't be as savvy as the Boss about how to get others to do want he wants, still, his strong desires and persistence may carry him over the top.

Very often one type is the precursor of the next. For example, a child who begins life lashing out in threatening situations (a Naysayer) may evolve into a Strong-Willed Child who uses his natural drive to get what he needs, but with less aggression or insensitivity. With good parental guidance and peer influence, he may gain leadership abilities and develop aspects of a Team Player. In this example he could turn out to be an active athletic type, able to play by the rules, but charismatic enough to lead the group in the direction it needs to go.

Expect your child's social style to evolve as she moves through life. Toddlers and preschoolers (see Chapters Four and Five) are still struggling with the basic tasks of getting to know themselves, and discovering the world. You'll find that your younger child is pretty rooted to one social style, but over time, as other facets of her personality emerge, frequently, an adaptive blend develops. For example, your child may be a Fragile Flower, who constantly worries about things going wrong. But as she gains a little more life experience, she may also be filled with an ability to drown her anxieties in her genuine delight at accomplishing new feats and in being part of the group. She is evolving into a blend of Team

Player/Fragile Flower, with the former predominating. The aware parent can help a child temper her traits by providing an environment that cultivates her strengths while deemphasizing her weaknesses.

KIDS BRING OUT EACH OTHER'S
STRENGTHS AND WEAKNESSES

It isn't only parents who shape a child's social skills. Over the years a child will form bonds with kids who have a range of different styles.

Let's see how this works. Ann, at nine, is a Shy Child and a Thinker with a healthy sense of self who is rather slow to adapt to new situations. She doesn't mind if other kids don't warm up to her immediately. As a matter of fact she has a pretty good ability to see things from someone else's point of view. And she can be motivated to get involved in an activity if other children give her a little encouragement.

Elaine, nine and a half, is a Strong-Willed Team Player, who often needs to have her own way, but she still has a positive approach to life. She tends to be a leader, and it's easy for her to get other kids organized.

These two were made for each other because they have attributes that really complement each other. Elaine overcomes Ann's hesitant approach and gets her involved. Then Ann starts having a great time. When Elaine gets surly or frustrated, Ann clicks into her friend's mood, offering understanding and compassion. Elaine lightens up because she feels she has a pal who really listens to her.

YOU CAN BOOST YOUR CHILD'S SOCIAL INTELLIGENCE

In subsequent chapters we will offer detailed strategies to help enhance your child's social intelligence. But there are a few general guidelines that you should keep in mind:

- **A parent can clarify for his child what's going on in a group.**

Steve's father noticed that his son would join a group just when they were disbanding, or he'd try to get a kid to play when that child was in the middle of a temper tantrum and wasn't in the mood.

He began spending some time in the playground with Steve and would occasionally offer suggestions on joining a group. He also helped Steve develop empathy skills by pointing out what different kids were feeling in a given situation so that Steve could get a better idea of others' feelings (see "Develop Your Empathy Energy," Chapter Seven) and time his social overtures better.

- **A parent can use structured play with her child to work out friendship issues.**

Dana's mother noted that her Strong-Willed daughter often insisted on getting her own way during a playdate. In order to get Dana to give a little more in a relationship, she practiced playing Simon Says to give Dana experience following and leading. She also encouraged her daughter to enact imaginary scenes of being with a friend by using dolls and puppets.

- **A parent can require more of his child.**

Don was always picking fights with other five-year-olds. His mother decided to help make him feel more responsible for others by assigning him the chore of feeding the pets each night. Praised for doing his daily task, Don started feeling really good about himself. This allowed him to concentrate less on his own needs in a group situation and to be more tolerant of his friends' behavior.

- **A parent can emphasize his child's strongest skills.**

Alice's mom knew that her reticent eight-year-old had trouble even thinking about being a leader, but that in time she could become the empathic core of a group or its effective peacemaker. Alice's mother suggested that her child ask a couple of the kids from a group she wanted to join for individual playdates. Because they said yes to her, she felt a little braver about joining their group. Whenever her mother saw Alice hanging back after that, she reminded her of how well her "single date" technique had worked before.

• **A parent can champion her child's friendships.**

We need to assure our children that their instincts for friendships are right and good. We need to appreciate their choices—even when they're not the choices we would have made.

With a new appreciation for your child's unique qualities, in most cases, you can make a difference in your child's social intelligence. Remember that in this realm, as in every other, practice makes better—if not perfect. Almost every child can learn to be a good friend and to accept the friendship of others.

In later chapters we'll discuss each age group separately so that we can help you along each step of the way to increase your child's empathy for others and enhance his ability to cope well with individuals or in a group. Throughout the book we'll point the way toward recognizing those golden opportunities.

Before you can help your child with his friendship skills, however, you must understand your own take on relationships. A thorough grounding in your friendship history will help you guide your child as he connects with friends, making bonds that will be with him for a rich, long lifetime.

3

YOUR PARENTING STYLE: A COMBINATION OF YOUR PAST AND YOUR PRESENT

Do you remember this scene?

You are standing near the bleachers behind the softball diamond, glove in hand. You've just moved here from another town. One kid on the team says, "Let's let the new kid play a while. He can't be any worse than some of the other lamebrains we've let in." *Success.*

Or this one?

Your best friend was supposed to wait for you on the corner. When you get there, she is deep in conversation with another girl. As you approach, they look directly at you and start giggling. *Failure.*

Or this one?

You are very small, trying to jump up to get on the swing. A big kid comes along and says he'll help get you up—if you promise to carry his backpack to school every day for the next week. You agree. He hoists you up effortlessly, then gives you the push you've waited for all your life. And as you are in orbit, he reaches up and yanks you off. You fall, skinning your knee. The big kid slaps you on the back and congratulates you on being such a good sport. *Success? Failure? Who can tell?*

You undoubtedly recall vivid scenes like these from your childhood. Some you remember with joy, some with acute pain.

In this chapter we'd like to help you avoid the major pitfall that many parents make, which is to assume that your child needs what you needed when you were little. In reality you and your child are two distinct individuals with two unique friendship histories.

Your child's personality may be completely different from yours. It's always interesting to see a pair of quiet academic couch potatoes who think a game of chess is an exciting social interaction who have a child of a totally different social style. She is bubbling over with physical energy, can't stay still a minute, and would rather jump on the bed than sleep in it. It almost looks like a genetic glitch—nature seemed to switch the logical baby for this couple with another made from an entirely different brew.

And we will hope that her parents understand that their child needs a different type of care, comforting, and discipline than they did as children. Our initial tendency is usually to parent our children as *we* needed to be parented. It's a natural mistake to make, but our trying to relive or revise the past doesn't help our children unless our parenting is suited to *their* unique needs. We have to identify, but not overidentify, with them.

By remembering to the best of your ability how you handled your early friendships, you will be able to compare and contrast them with those your own child is currently experiencing. And by recognizing who you are now, you can gain a better perspective on your parenting.

MOTIVATIONS—YOUR OWN AND YOUR CHILD'S

Why do you want your child to make friends? This may seem like a simplistic question, but when you think about it, you'll probably come up with a lot of answers. Of course you want your son or daughter to mix and mingle easily, because you know there are so many occasions in life when getting along is paramount to doing well: at school, on a team, in a playground, in an office, in a marriage. And the better your child gets along—by himself, with one individual or with many—the more comfortable he'll be in the world.

But maybe there are additional reasons that have more to do with you and your friendship history than with your child. Perhaps you fear that your child *won't* be accepted, because of either her social style or her social skills or even how she dresses or where she lives. How does this reflect on you?

Perhaps you fear that your child will be better accepted than you ever were. You may have always felt like a loner, on the outskirts of all the fun. And you see your child growing into a real social butterfly. Are you jealous? Are you annoyed at what you consider the superficiality of her relationships? How do you think this reflects on you?

If you *do* think it reflects on you, you may be losing some perspective on where you stand in relation to your child. As her parent you must learn to pick out her strengths and weaknesses, differentiate them from yours, and help only in a way that will be most beneficial to her, even if that help is standing back silently and just supporting.

THE CORNERSTONES OF PARENTING FOR GOOD FRIENDSHIPS

Since the family circle is the seat of all our basic emotions and reactions, what happens in the home environment affects how our children deal with the world. Parents are the first teachers of social interaction. After parents come grandparents and other close family, teachers, baby-sitters, neighbors, and a wide range of acquaintances and friends.

We can do our kids a great service by opening up the rest of the world for them. By allowing our children contact with others who may not share our beliefs or ideals, we give them the opportunity to compare and contrast life-styles. When your child is able to differentiate "the way *we* do things at home" from everything else, she has a rich mix of options to pick from.

But what is "home-style" exactly? The following five parental influences may be the most significant in our children's early social development:

1. **Modeling.** The way that you conduct your marital or partnership relationship has a significant bearing on your child's friendships. It's to be hoped that you and your mate are friends as well as romantic partners; you developed an intimate relationship together because you liked *and* loved each other. Your child sees a duo learning to balance wants and needs. Your children pay close attention to the way you conduct your friendships. If they see good, loving relationships that give you and others lots of pleasure, if they see you resolving differences and negotiating wants and needs, they'll understand that friendship is an important element in their lives too.

If you are divorced or a single parent, your child will be influenced by how you develop relationships with others of both sexes. And if you have extended family around you, you will also be modeling friendships for your children when they see how you deal with your siblings and your own parents.

2. **Communication.** The way that you respond to your child emotionally—as a good listener who is giving and

open or as a less understanding person who tends to be rather brusque—will affect your child's interactions with others.

3. **Parenting style.** You may be pretty strict and insist on your child toeing the mark; you may be very liberal and permissive about rules; or you may be both warm and authoritative in your approach. The way in which you parent helps to structure your child's friendship too.

4. **Combined history.** Together you and your partner have a lot of friendship history. This can help or hurt your child because of the myriad feelings and expectations involved, and that's why it's important to be very clear about your own ability to interact with others and about the way you'd like your child to do it.

5. **Environment.** You make all the physical decisions that determine your child's early social contacts. You pick a certain house or apartment to live in that could be miles from civilization or right on top of dozens of neighbors. You join a playgroup or a day-care facility. You hire baby-sitters and invite families over for dinner. The way that you manage the first years of your child's life has a great bearing on who she meets and how often she comes into contact with others.

These five influences are crucial to the way your family functions as a social unit. Now, in order to understand how you as a parent use these elements, let's examine in detail your unique approach to friendship.

YOUR SOCIAL-HISTORY QUESTIONNAIRE

You are now going to take an excursion back in time to your childhood. The Social-History Questionnaire that follows is intended to jog your memories about how you reacted to your own past and then to bring you up-to-date on your present friendships.

Remember when . . .

1. Did you consider your parents good friends with each other? If so, why? If not, why not?

2. How were you punished when you were little? Did you consider your parents strict or liberal?

3. What are your first friendship memories, both bad and good?

4. Did you consider yourself an outsider, longing to get in? Why?

5. Was there ever a time when you desperately wanted to be someone's friend or belong to some group and couldn't? What did you think you had done to become excluded?

6. Did you see yourself as popular? Belonging to one group or several?

7. What conscious steps or manuevers did you take to be liked by a certain person or group?

8. Did you ever have a best friend? How old were you and how long did that friendship last? What ended it? Or cooled it to just an ordinary friendship?

9. Did your parents generally like your friends or dislike them?

10. Did your parents try to select your friends?

11. Did your parents allow you to do things your friends did?

12. What did you expect of a friend?

13. Did you have good friends mostly of the same sex? Of the opposite sex?

14. What do you think your friends would have said about your capacity for friendship?

15. Are you still friendly with people you knew as children? How have those friendships changed over the years?

Comparing past and present . . .

16. When you were six, did you select friends who led you around or whom you could lead around? Or did you have a mix?

- What about at ten?
- In your teen years?
- Today do you prefer friends who allow you to be the leader or those who expect you to be the follower? Do you have some of each?

17. When you were six, did you have one or two good friends or many friends?

- When you were ten, did that change?
- How about when you were a teenager?
- How about today? How many friends have you kept from childhood, from school, from your first adult living and working situation?

18. When you were six, did you always want to take your ball and go home after a fight? Did you give in quickly, hoping the other child would like you better? Or did you battle it out to the bitter end?

- How did you handle arguments when you were ten? When you were a teenager? Do you recall giving a little more, accepting your friends' differences a little better?
- How do you handle dissent today? Do you blow up at a friend, stay mad for a few hours, then call and try to work it out? Do you simmer for weeks, then finally explode at something else that has nothing to do with the real issue? Do you consider an occasional altercation a reasonable part of a friendship? Of your relationship with your partner?

How do you see your child in her own friendship stage right now? If you're an outgoing individual who felt excluded from many groups as a child, you may project your concerns onto your child and worry that she might be going through the same kind of experience. But suppose you have the kind of kid who really enjoys spending a few afternoons alone with a book? She may not have the same impression of friendship that you do. To her, being alone does not necessarily mean being lonely. Always stop and think before you make assumptions about your child.

YOUR PARENTING STYLE

Your parenting style is largely determined by the way you set limits and show compassion. Some parents demand total respect and authority; some are completely laissez-faire and feel that a child grows most naturally when she learns to make her own choices. Most of us fall somewhere in the middle of this continuum. The ideal parenting style blends *empathy* and *control.*

Why is this so? Because we learn first in the safest setting—the home—that life is all about give-and-take. A child who feels that his parent can really empathize (feel what *he* is feeling) will develop a close relationship with that parent and be more willing to accept having limits set for him. He is also more likely to carry that empathy into a friendship. If he sees his mother and father sharing with each other and with friends and family in an altruistic way, he learns that kindness and openness feel good.

But a child also needs limits to be set for him by an older, wiser individual. In time he gains the ability to transfer these to a friendship—and becomes able to give up something of his own when a friend really wants or needs it.

A child who isn't corrected when he snatches a toy away from another child or calls a friend stupid is going to have a hard time making and keeping friends in the future. To be good friends, children need to know how to see someone else's point of view, how to compromise, how to share, how to give.

They learn these important lessons, in great part, from parents who insist that their kids exert some age-appropriate self-control over their wants and needs. No matter how old we are, we can't maintain a friendship without both give and take.

The first step for parents who care about fostering this skill is to encourage the desire to reach out to others. Surprisingly the way to do this is not just to provide a role model as an understanding, all-forgiving parent. If you do everything for your child and allow him to take without limitations, he will assume that everything he wants just comes to him. He will think that he has no obligation to give back.

But by setting clear limits—the rules and regulations of human relations—parents teach children to share, to cooperate, and to help. These behaviors require some selflessness and self-discipline—qualities that usually require years of practice. We must nourish these in our kids if their efforts at establishing relationships are to be welcomed by those they meet.

Dr. Diana Baumrind, one of the influential thinkers in family development, felt that there were three types of parents: the *authoritarian* parent, who scored high in control and low in warmth; the *authoritative* parent, who scored high in both control and warmth; and the *permissive* parent, who scored high in warmth but low in control. Baumrind discovered that an authoritative parent was the most effective of the three because he established a good balance between setting limits and responding emotionally to his child.

I have expanded Baumrind's three parenting types by filling in the continuum that stretches from the most strict and controlling to the most laissez-faire parent, as follows:

Tough Guy——Firm Guider——Understander——Worrier——Inconsistent Parent

On the left side we have the strictest parent, who feels that control is the most important aspect of parenting. The Tough Guy discourages his child from "talking back," even from explaining when he's done something wrong, and the child gets the feeling that trying to be "good" is useless since he's so "bad" all the time. Unfortunately this authoritarian parent often seems arbitrary and unfair, and the child can't feel that his parent is guiding out of love. Usually the Tough Guy disciplines with contempt, belittling the child who's "done wrong." He may have been treated like an inferior in his own childhood and tends to be cut off from any feelings of low self-esteem in himself because they are too painful to deal with. He therefore projects his low self-esteem onto others. This type of parent must get help to understand the causes of his anger so he can parent more appropriately. Otherwise, his child will become angry with himself, his parent, and the world.

The firm but kind parent—the Understander and the Firm Guider—maintains control over a child in a far different way, demanding maturity and independence over rote performance of duties and obligations. This authoritative parent exudes a sense of law and order, but it's mitigated by warmth and compassion. It's a blend of empathy and control.

The Firm Guider uses her power as a parent in a positive manner, listening to her child's side in an argument, then quickly deciding whether it needs to be challenged. She tends to be higher on setting limits than understanding. Her matter-of-fact approach to discipline is usually helpful—for example, assigning room cleanup for a week in order to punish her nine-year-old for a mess left in the room. She has a certain flexibility that allows her to attend to her child's needs, and if she functions effectively, she is able to offer a good blend of separateness and togetherness.

The Understander is a sympathetic person, a very good listener who is able to think about all sides of an issue. An Understander's first response is empathy with her child, although in many situations she can be understanding of others as well and can help her child to see a different point of view. She may be so quick to see another's perspective that she neglects her own and thus may find it difficult to discipline and control when needed. The understanding parent is sometimes not up to the task of giving an older child something to resist, something "real" against which to define himself, particularly as he encounters more situations in life that require him to take a definite stand.

The Worrier and the Inconsistent Parent waffle on when they should be empathic and when they should control. Their children may be restricted or allowed to run free at different times, because the parents are unsure about parenting.

The Worrier is an anxious parent. He is *overly* concerned about his child's welfare, to the extent that he takes the child's problems as his own and becomes depressed if they can't be worked out. He may forbid his child to cross the street because he thinks something terrible might happen, and consequently his child will grow up apprehensive about any new experience. Or he may allow his child to cross the street, but put so many restrictions on him that the child still feels hampered. A Worrier is often a hypochondriac on behalf of his child, keeping his son or daughter home from school for the least sniffle or bump. This parent needs help either from his partner and friends or through counseling, so as not to project his anxieties onto his child.

The Inconsistent Parent is easily manipulated by her child. This individual usually doesn't have a positive sense of herself and therefore feels unable to guide her child. She puts up with a lot of shenaningans before reaching a boiling point. The result of this is that the child is usually confused about his behavior, realizing that he's over the line but lacking respect for the parent who gives him no limitations. He may become whiny and ungiving. This parent may be very high on the warmth meter, but probably doesn't demand enough from her child. This parent needs to be more strong-willed and develop a more clearly defined sense of self. She needs to feel she has a right to make rules and decisions whenever needed.

Examine the parenting chart on page 63, and see where you fall in the range of control-to-responsiveness.

Naturally there are gradations of all these categories—sometimes we fall more on one side than on another. But studies indicate that the closer you can get to the center, the better for your child. The child of a Tough Guy tends to act hostile and aggressive when friends don't behave the way he wants; the child of an Inconsistent Parent or a Worrier tends either to take advantage of friends or feel inadequate to cope in a social setting. The parent or parents who are at either extreme (too authoritarian or too permissive) tend to have children who have trouble with self-control and alignment in a group.

But the child of an Understander or a Firm Guider, or a marriage between these two, is guided by a good mix of *empathy* and *control*. This allows the child to feel comfortable and secure, ready to take on the outside world.

WHAT KIND OF PARENT ARE YOU?

Identify your own parenting style and your partner's on the chart, and try to understand the nuances of each. For example, are you basically an Understander, doing a great job on the whole but needing to be just a bit firmer? Maybe under stress you tend to become a Worrier and lose your ability to separate yourself emotionally from your child. In order to boost your parenting rating (see chart), you may want to require more of your child—more appropriate chores and

PARENTING SKILLS

Parenting Type	Has Compassion for Child's Feelings	Is Sufficiently Emotionally Separate	Analyzes Situations and Thinks Developmentally	Requires Child to Do Appropriate Chores	Requires Child to Think of Others
Tough Guy	△	△	△	○	□
Firm Guider	□	□	□	○	○
Understander	○	□	○	△	△
Worrier	○	△	□	△	△
Inconsistent Parent	○	△	△	△	△

○ high ability　□ medium ability　△ low ability

more consideration of others. Once you have a good handle on your parenting abilities, you can become a better model and guide for your child.

ONE FAMILY'S STORY

The parenting styles that you and your partner combine add yet another dimension to your family. Think about Dee and Jim, and their eight-year-old son, Peter. Mom is the life of every party, on every town committee. People naturally gravitate toward her—she can organize a group without even seeming to make an attempt. She doesn't have a lot of close friends—never did—but that doesn't bother her. She runs a tight parenting ship, definitely a Tough Guy when it comes to running the household. It's not just that she doesn't let Peter get away with murder—she won't even let him escape for a minor misdemeanor.

Peter's dad, Jim, has a wonderful ability to analyze situations and make peace in conflict. He has three close friends he's kept since childhood—one is a woman—and they see each other regularly. He's understanding, very laissez-faire, and might be classified as an Inconsistent Parent. Peter always goes to him when he thinks he's going to get in trouble with Mom. He knows his father is a terrific listener, and sometimes Jim can persuade Dee that she ought to soften her discipline style.

Dee and Jim have a good relationship, though her hair-trigger temper doesn't mesh well with Jim's brooding silences. Peter has always been careful of his mother, and he tends to be the same around dominating friends. But he's picked a best friend who is more like him. Right now Peter is struggling with his desire to stick with his one best friend versus the pressures on him from school and Mom to "join a team and play the field."

It will be interesting to see whether Peter becomes more or less gregarious over time. If his mother is able to moderate her bossy behavior a bit and his father is willing to assume more control, Peter might find that his sense of himself grows stronger, because he will feel more firm support from his parents. When he can be less preoccupied with whether or not he can get his needs taken care of at home, he may find it easier to reach out to a variety of others while still maintaining his loyalties to close friends.

BE EMPATHIC BUT DON'T PROJECT

It's important to distinguish the feelings you recall from your own childhood from those you think your child has now. Remember that the best models and coaches combine warmth with power, limit-setting with compassion. Follow the suggestions below for better parenting on friendship issues *without interference from your own past*:

1. Sit down with your child and listen carefully when she wants to talk about friendship issues. Be certain she is listening when you're explaining things to her. Very young children won't be able to grasp another person's perspective, but they will learn to communicate more effectively if you give them lots of practice in how it's done.

2. Empathize, but then step back emotionally. Wait and observe the skills your child is using or not using in the situation.

3. Stop and ask yourself, knowing your child's social style and your own, whether you may be projecting your own fears and humiliations on the scene or whether you are simply feeling deeply for your child.

4. Stop and ask yourself what your child might do to resolve the problem. Remember that if you intervene right

away, he will not get a chance to experiment with social skills he may have the potential to develop.

5. If you still feel you must intervene, do not immediately lend your child the skills you use so well (both from your own social style and your greater life experience). Your skills may be totally inappropriate to his needs. Before you rush in, think about who he is, what his skills and potential skills are, and only then suggest something appropriate to him.

6. Don't be afraid to be angry occasionally at your partner in front of your child. As long as you both aren't overwhelmingly furious and yelling isn't a household pattern, there's nothing wrong in her seeing you argue. It's good for her to understand that friends can fight and make up.

7. Don't expect too much. Children can be cruel, and they can change allegiance with lightning speed. Allow your child to have and give disappointments. Nobody's perfect.

8. Allow your child to approach the outside world with confidence. If you are too strict or too liberal in the home setting, your son or daughter will have more trouble feeling they can find their way into and out of groups without you.

9. Coach your child so that he can learn to handle a problem by himself the next time. This means helping your child assess his own reactions to a situation and letting him develop appropriate responses. You can try to get him to take the focus off his own misery by offering him the other child's perspective; or you can remind him of another time when he got angry and made up with a friend or was excluded and later included in a group.

10. Finally remember that it's not your job to "fix" all the bad parts of a relationship, even if your child asks you to do so. And children have a greater flexibility than most grown-ups. They can hate and loathe a friend one day and swear they'll never speak again, then be bosom buddies twenty-four hours later.

USING YOUR SELF-KNOWLEDGE
TO ENHANCE YOUR CHILD'S POTENTIAL

Now that you're aware of your own parenting style and can see how your fix on friendship differs from that of your child, you will be much more adept at recognizing and encouraging his social potential. In the following chapters, as we take you from one age group to the next, you will be able to use your self-knowledge to play with your child, listen when he needs your ear, and support him in all the exciting friendship experiences he has before him.

4

FRIENDSHIP AMONG CHILDREN AGES EIGHTEEN MONTHS TO THREE YEARS

"Doggie for me. Bear for me. Blankie for me." Two-year-old Mike walked around the playground systematically gathering up the other children's toys. The owners either looked at him in stunned amazement or tried to grab them back. Mike's mother came over and gently pried the items out of her son's hand, but he shook his head. "No! Mine!" She kept trying to explain, but couldn't make him understand that these things belonged to the other children.

"Mommy, want Mommy!" Nineteen-month-old Karen was inconsolable every day when her mother left her at the day-care center. And yet, the teacher told Karen's mother, she was perfectly fine a few minutes later when Sueanne, a very outgoing toddler in the group, came over and took Karen's hand.

"Cars going fast! Watch out!" Lauren, who was nearly three, scooted her toy cars along the floor. "Zoom!" she yelled. Sarah, who had just turned three, kept tugging at her doll's dress, trying to get it off.

"Dollie, dollie, play with me," she sang. Lauren's mother could see that the two girls didn't mind *one another's company, but they didn't seem to relate at all. They each had their stuff and didn't want to share. There seemed to be some connection between them, but she couldn't figure out what it was.*

MOVING OUT FROM HOME BASE:
A CHILD'S FIRST SOCIAL CONTACT

The social activity of a very young child is just beginning to play a big part in her life. If your child has started day care or some kind of playgroup—as many kids do at this age— her world will open up from the warm security of home to include playmates and other caregivers.

You and your partner were probably your baby's primary source of stimulation for the first year and a half, and that's as it should be. Of course, aside from a mother, father, and siblings, an infant may have grandparents, aunts and uncles, baby-sitters, neighbors, and others who are part of her life. Basically, however, family bonding is paramount for an infant.

At about eighteen months, however, something changes. Whereas the baby perceives her parents as an extension of herself, the toddler can begin to differentiate her own identity from that of her mother and father. Another important developmental step is the mastery of a rudimentary vocabulary. A child learns that words help her to communicate with others and that she can negotiate her own needs.

It can be hard for a parent who has previously offered all the excitement in her child's life to be in any way supplanted by others. But as you will see, when your child moves out into the world—scary as this may be for both of you!— she has the best chance of becoming a well-rounded, socially active individual. And the comparison she soon will be able to make about the way "we" do things and "they" do things is an important distinction to master. Once a child can see that every family is not just like hers and that people do and say things differently, she can develop a keener appreciation for her own environment.

HOW YOUR CHILD GROWS SOCIALLY
FROM EIGHTEEN MONTHS TO THREE YEARS

Children with different social styles naturally glean different elements from this time of their lives. For the extroverts—the Team Player, the Boss, the Performer, the Strong-Willed Child, or the Adapter—this can be a time of fury and passion as they try to include others into what used to be their own personal world. The blossoming of a strong ego takes place at this stage for extroverted children, and while their newborn sense of self will help them feel confident out in the world, the transition is sometimes rocky.

The introverts—the Follower, the Fragile Flower, the Shy Child, the Thinker, and the Naysayer—may find new situations frightening or intimidating. But if you can prepare them in advance for social events, each subsequent one may become easier and more enjoyable. Since introverts generally cope better in a one-on-one situation, you may want to concentrate on playdates with one other child as opposed to large groups.

WHAT ISSUES ARE PARAMOUNT
FOR YOUR CHILD RIGHT NOW?

The main friendship issues for this age group are:

- The child defining herself in relation to others
- Separation anxiety—parents versus everyone else

- Parallel play—the beginning of sharing
- Learning to negotiate

Children in the eighteen-month to three-year-old age group are struggling to *define themselves in relation to others*. This means that their "things" belong to them and no one else. It can be tough to see your child fighting with other kids over possessions. But she knows her world and the parts of it that belong to her, and she isn't about to give them up. This new distinction about who she is and what she owns is pretty crudely formed, so it may set off a lot of battles over turf.

Many children start some form of day care at this stage, whether home-based or out in the world, and this can cause *separation anxiety*. Nervousness about leaving home and parents can trigger a variety of concerns, which may sometimes be more difficult for Mom and Dad than for the child!

An interesting corollary to anxiety over separation is parent substitution. Your child craves a replacement for the parent who isn't around, and this desire can foster *parallel play* with another child. Playing alongside someone else is the entrée to good socialization.

Even playing beside another individual who has his own wants and needs, however, can be tough for children in this egocentric stage of life. Parents must be able to tolerate their child's early attempts to sort out his identity from others' and then must step in to help teach *beginning negotiation skills*.

In order for you to understand what your child is feeling, you must be able to enter her world and really hear what goes on inside it. Children communicate through play, so understanding what happens in their play will help you to nurture good friendship skills.

In my work with parents, I've found that helping them develop certain types of listening skills can be very useful. I've adapted these techniques into Social Skills Play Kits. These kits offer you ways to observe and listen to your child so that you can help her make sense of her world as she explores it. You can use what you discover together to clear up difficult issues, allay fears, and make your child feel more at ease in any social situation. As you practice giving and taking together in play, you'll be able to bring out your child's potential with various social skills.

Very young children aren't going to be able to tell you what's on their minds or why they aren't getting along well with their friends. That's why this Social Skills Play Kit for parents of children from eighteen months to about six years of age uses toys and objects you probably have around the house. If you have the right play equipment on hand when you need it, you'll be able to help your young child with important friendship issues.

PLAY-KIT MATERIALS FOR YOUR YOUNG CHILD

You'll probably want to expand this Social Skills Play Kit as your child's social style evolves and different skills need to be worked on. But for now here's a basic list of the toys and materials I recommend:

1. A dollhouse with furniture, cars, and people who represent your family and your child's friends.
2. A schoolhouse/day-care center.
3. A playground (this can be a piece of cardboard with some improvised swings made of string and bits of cardboard).

4. Roads and sidewalks, also cardboard.
5. A doctor/dentist office/hospital.
6. A store.
7. Balls or sticks of different colors.
8. A set of hand puppets representing family and friends.
9. A toy clock with movable hands.
10. A book of photographs. You may use pictures of your child and cut out pictures from magazines of people with different emotional expressions. These pictures can be placed in a binder.
11. A series of pictures of your child with his friends. This will serve as a jumping-off point for various stories he'll make up at different times.
12. Items that have been personalized with your child's name to reinforce identity—a towel, a set of pencils, a wall-hook panel, some stationery.

HOW TO USE YOUR KIT

These materials will give you the opportunity to work on social skills that may be weak or missing, or to find out what's wrong in a particular social situation. For example, if your toddler always hits other children to get a toy, you might look at the pictures of himself and his friends and have him try to identify the expression that most nearly matches what he feels when he wants to hit someone. If he picks "sad" or "angry," you can then discuss with him how it feels to be sad or angry. Getting him to put feelings into words will help him to stop hitting and to try new ways of getting along with others.

Suppose she's having a separation problem in nursery school. Ask your child to make up a story about her day using the doll-house, roads, and school. You can verbalize some of her feelings for her if she gets stuck—just make very sure you don't superimpose *your* feelings on top of hers. When she acts out what's going on in her life, you'll be able to see what upsets her. This technique will also allow her to feel your interest and love because you're paying a lot of attention to *her* feelings. Together you can help her cope with her difficulties and possibly try new ways to separate that will make her feel better.

When she's a little older, you can use the Social Skills Play Kit to help her role-play different outcomes for the same situation. As she experiments with emotions by changing her feelings and perhaps also changing the feelings of the children she's pretending to play with, her abilities to empathize and be considerate of others will be enhanced.

DEFINING HIMSELF:
"No! Mine! Give it back!"

"Gimme truck! Mine!" screamed two-year-old Sam in the middle of the park. Sam, a Boss in most situations, but acting more and more like a Fragile Flower these days, lunged toward the little boy beside him, pushed him roughly, then grabbed the fire truck the child was holding. The other little boy shoved back, retrieved his truck, and punched Sam's arm. Sam shrank from his attacker, and his wails of anguish echoed around the playground. Sam's father threw up his hands. Why did this happen every single day, with every child Sam met?

He took Sam in his arms and tried to explain that the truck didn't belong to him and that if he asked nicely, maybe the other little boy would let him play with it for a while. But Sam refused to be consoled. "No, MINE! Give it back!" he kept screaming. Totally frustrated by the tantrum, his father finally picked Sam up, still screaming, and lugged him back to the car.

What's Really Going On?

Sam is struggling to define himself in relation to the world. He is not developmentally ready to learn that other people have priorities that don't match his. He certainly cannot understand his father's insistence that the fire truck "belongs to" another child. To his way of thinking anything within his immediate province is his.

Sam's father is confused by the fact that although Sam is clearly a Boss, always trying to get other people to do things, he also behaves like an introverted Fragile Flower, backing away from the conflict he's started. It's not at all unusual for a two-year-old to show a mix of these two, seemingly opposite qualities. What's predominant in a two-year-old's personality is the issue of self-definition. This means that, first, he demands his way no matter what and, second, he takes everything personally. Hence the so-called Terrible Twos, where tantrums are sometimes more common than settled behavior.

Sam's sense of self is consolidating now, and one of the consequences of figuring out just who he is is that he cannot share his stuff with anyone else. If Sam were more of an introvert, perhaps a Thinker or a Shy Child, he probably wouldn't pursue the boy with the fire truck, but he might sulk and complain to his mother to get it for him. An Adapter of this age might be perfectly happy with any other toy that a parent presented as an alternative to the truck he wasn't allowed to keep.

Two characteristics of a child of this age are that he likes things the way they are, and he values his possessions highly. These possessions will play an increasingly important role in his socialization as he grows. As you will see in Chapter Six, the five-to-seven-year-old uses concrete items like toys and food as bartering tools to get other kids' attention and approval. Later, at about age eight, possessions will be replaced by abstract qualities—kids at that age are able to exchange concern, support, and understanding.

We all have to start somewhere, however, and it's appropriate for a child in this age group to learn to separate himself from others by identifying (sometimes at the top of his lungs!) what he owns and what they own. So don't worry that his hawklike devotion to material possessions means he will necessarily turn into a stingy, ungiving individual who can't open up to others. First he has to define himself and his world. Only then will he have the self-confidence to include others in his world and venture out into their worlds as well.

Your Child/Your Role

HAS YOUR CHILD EVER:

- Grabbed a toy away from a playmate and refused to give it back?
- Insisted that she bring all her "things"—stuffed toy, blanket, boots, a favorite pair of barrettes—to a playdate with another child?
- Compared body parts with a friend—pointing at his nose, then his friend's nose, and saying about both, "Mine!"

How You Can Encourage Appropriate Social Skills

The social skills you want to develop around the issue of self-definition are very basic. You want to encourage your child to participate with others willingly, to have a sense of enthusiasm for whatever he's doing, and, if possible, an ability to maintain group activities, even if he can't follow the rules just yet. In other words, you want to try to make his self-definition clearer by juxtaposing him with others. Seeing the *other* allows him to understand who *he* is.

To help your child make the distinction between his things and someone else's, use your Social Skills Play Kit to play a turn-taking game. You can assign one group of toys to your child and one to yourself. Ask your child to put one of his objects inside the dollhouse, then you'll put in one of yours. Understanding the concept of "first yours, then mine" with a trusted parent can open your child to share better with friends.

Next you can play a sorting game. If your child already knows colors, have him put all the blue toys in one pile, all the green toys in another, and the red toys in a third. Or you can sort silverware—ask your child to put the spoons, forks, and knives in their appropriate slots. You can sort laundry too—all the dark clothes in one pile, all the light clothes in another. This will teach your child to see the difference between groups. Understanding the distinction between groups of items is the another important step in teaching your child the concept of "mine versus yours."

The next step is to teach him that certain things belong to him whereas others belong to his friends. Go back to your play kit and pick out several play figures that represent him and his friends. Color-code a variety of toys with stick-on color dots. Sam's toys can be all green, his friend Bill's all blue, and so on. When the colors have been assigned, give a red toy to a green-toy child and ask Sam if you've done it right. If not, have him correct the mistake.

Finally you can suggest that your child take away some of the red child's toys. Use your photo album and have him pick an emotion picture (angry, sad, indignant, and so on) indicating how the friend would feel when his things are taken away.

You can work on these games with your kit for several minutes each day, but it's also helpful to take your skills out into the real world. You might want to consider joining a playgroup with your child. Playgroups are beneficial because they provide social continuity—the kids get to see the same faces on a weekly basis. Also, this is an opportunity for your child to see you in a social setting. By watching Mom or Dad modeling good participatory skills, your child will get the idea that this is what he's supposed to do. You and another parent set up the picnic table and chairs in the yard; he and another boy mimic this by arranging the cardboard bricks in a row.

Because keeping things "homey" is important to a child of this age, you'll probably want to rotate the playgroup from one house to the next. (Also, no one parent would want their home invaded by eight or ten toddlers on a weekly basis!) This experience provides your child with a feeling of sameness (his own place) and newness (all the other houses and toys). And it gives him the opportunity, however crudely developed, to be a host sometimes and a guest sometimes.

The issue of "me" and "mine" will come up frequently for your toddler. Again, use your Social Skills Play Kit to help your child figure out who "me" is. If you have a monogrammed baby cup, take it out of storage and let him use it as a crayon holder. Putting up a sign with his name on his bedroom door or buying him a personalized bath towel will also help him define himself in relation to others and solidify the idea that he is a social being.

SEPARATION ANXIETY:
"Don't leave me, Mommy— I hate when you leave me!"

Jeff was an Adapter, but his parents saw that he was becoming a blend of social styles that definitely included Thinker. He and Nicole, another nineteen-month-old, had playdates every Friday morning while their mothers collaborated on a children's book they were trying to write. The two children would have a snack, play with toys and run around, have a nap, and then the mothers would take them to the park in their strollers.

On one particular Friday Jeff's mother asked a sitter to come in because she had a dentist's appointment right after the playdate. She waved good-bye to her son and walked to the elevator with Nicole and Nicole's mom. Jeff, who until that time had been happily pitching Legos at the living-room wall, suddenly burst into tears and ran down the hall toward the departing group, screaming, "Don't leave me, Mommy. I hate when you leave me!"

The next Friday, when Nicole and her mom arrived, Jeff began crying again and trailed his mother around the apartment for the remainder of the playdate.

What's Really Going On?

Jeff has made a connection between his mother's leaving him and seeing Nicole. Although he has obviously enjoyed playdates with her for some time, the wrenching sight of his mother disappearing with his friend into the elevator produced anxiety.

He's also concerned about his mother going off to be with another child. The fantasy of abandonment often accompanies anxiety over separation—Jeff might be thinking, "If she's going, she must be going to another kid she likes better than me." And after dealing with the fear of being left, Jeff has to deal with his feelings of jealousy toward Nicole, the lucky kid who got to leave the house with *his* mom.

In this scenario Jeff needed a clearer transition from being with his parent to being without his parent. His mom did not tell him that she'd be leaving, so he had no time to adjust to a new set of circumstances. This break in expectations was very hard for him.

The separation anxiety that takes place at ages two and

three is a hint of the existential aloneness we all feel, and it reemerges in adolescence. As you'll see in Chapter Eight, children from the ages of ten to twelve feel terribly confused about their struggle for independence. They still have a longing to be taken care of by their parents, yet they realize that we all must become separate and grow up.

We actually are never finished dealing with this issue. Many of us go through a mid-life crisis in our forties or fifties where we must cover the same territory yet again. And if it's terrifying for a mature, emotionally experienced adult to realize how alone she is in the world, imagine how scary this realization must be for a toddler!

Naturally the toddler has no real understanding of how life works, but only knows that self-reliance means losing the comfort of his parents' sheltering arms. Yet slowly learning to deal with the issue at this age can give a child a solid foundation for appreciating the real value of a friend later in life.

This is why playgroups with a parent present offer wonderful opportunities to learn to separate. Your child can run off to play with other kids and can still come back to you to touch base. You are there and not there at the same time.

Different types of children handle separation in different ways. Introverts tend to be self-reflective and blame themselves for their parents' leaving, even though they're not responsible for it. Extroverted kids, on the other hand, tend to handle separation better if another child is present to whom they can redirect their emotions. An extrovert can usually be persuaded by a sitter to engage in parallel play just about the time that a parent is leaving the scene. This kind of child may pay less attention to his parent's departure because he is easily stimulated by the prospect of starting a new activity with someone else.

The company of other kids gives your child an opportunity for a kind of attachment that is different from the one he has to you and your partner. He can find that it's more fun to follow and imitate certain other children, who then become his "favorites." There will be some kids he really likes, others he dislikes, and some about whom he couldn't care less. A lot of his choices depend on the social style of the other child and how it meshes or clashes with his.

Playmates can also provide relationships that are not quite so intense and frustrating as the parent-child bond. You may feel as if your whole day is built out of confrontations as you struggle to keep your cool in the face of your child's emphatic nos. But when your child separates from you in fury, he can get some temporary solace for feeling alone and abandoned by immediately connecting with another child.

Your Child/Your Role

HAS YOUR CHILD EVER:

- Refused to play with other children when you're away on a business trip?
- Hit another child after you've left the room?
- Seemed not to mind your departure, but then convinced his playmate that they should crayon all over the wall when the sitter wasn't looking?

How You Can Encourage Appropriate Social Skills

You'd like your eighteen-month-to-three-year-old to part smoothly and comfortably from you and go right to play. Your own comfort with separating is very important at this stage. If it's difficult for you to leave your son or daughter in someone else's care, it will be equally difficult for him to tolerate it. All kinds of fears about what might happen to your child when you're not around can begin to surface. Many children, particularly introverts, will pick up on their parents' anxious or guilty feelings and find separation intolerable.

But if you can see the light at the end of the tunnel (the second-grader who happily kisses you good-bye each morning as she races off to school, where she can see all her friends), you will relish the opportunity to encourage your child's socialization at this age. And you'll do much better with partings.

One important key to success is your ability to stimulate your child's interest in something other than you. You can wean your child away by leaving her with a "transitional object" (her favorite stuffed animal) or with another child whom she particularly likes. Some children may find it comforting to wave good-bye to you at the window as their caregiver holds them.

You might try rehearsing the good-bye. Practice with a sibling or a playmate at home as you explain to your child where you're going and what he's going to do when you're gone. Let's use Jeff's mother as an example. She could have asked Nicole and her mother to leave fifteen minutes early. This way all the important people wouldn't be leaving at once, giving Jeff the feeling that he was being abandoned. His mother might have used the Play Kit dollhouse and dentist office, explaining in a concrete way where she was going, and then used the toy clock to show when she would be back. This would have given Jeff time alone with his mother and made him feel calmer about their parting.

Some more extroverted children may not cry and carry on as Jeff did, but will find a different way to protest your not being with them. Some kids will appear to be happy and carefree, but as soon as you leave them, they will get involved in some "naughty" behavior—throwing food, coloring on the walls, losing their toilet training—that they would not typically do. The same preparatory process will work for them too.

PARALLEL PLAY:
"I sit and color. You too."

Emily was sitting with her mother in the pediatrician's waiting room. At three Emily was a Strong-Willed Child and a Performer, but she was pretty adaptable too. She quickly found all the best coloring books and crayons in the room and took up a station near the front door where she could check out the newcomers as she scribbled in the coloring book.

Another toddler, Jeremy, about twenty-four months old, came in with his father. Jeremy was a very Shy Child, often a Fragile Flower, and he looked pretty miserable sitting curled up next to his father on the sofa. Emily colored away and looked so happily absorbed that Jeremy's father took his son by the hand and placed him beside her. "Make friends," he said emphatically. Jeremy looked over at Emily's stash of crayons, but made no move to take any from her, to talk with her, or to interact with her in any way.

After a while Emily took one coloring book that she had finished using and placed it and one red crayon on the floor between her and Jeremy. Jeremy stared straight ahead.

Emily busily colored in her own book. "I sit and color," she stated. "You too." She didn't look at him or invite him to take the equipment, but the offer was clear enough. "Go ahead, Jeremy," his father urged. "The little girl wants you to play with her."

Eventually Jeremy picked up the crayon and started to color, but he paid absolutely no attention to Emily, nor did she seem to notice him.

What's Really Going On?

Emily, an extroverted, socially intelligent child, is reaching out to Jeremy in a very three-year-old way. Jeremy's father doesn't understand Emily's indirect method of communication, so he pushes for more contact between the children. Of course he's unsuccessful and gets no reaction from his son.

Children of this age are just honing their new social skills and shouldn't be expected to "make friends" with strangers or "go play." They really don't know what those terms mean. Jeremy doesn't feel better about his father's intervention—as a matter of fact his fragile sense of self may feel challenged by his father's insistence. He may feel bad enough already, having to go to the doctor, and this experience may highlight his feelings of being small and vulnerable.

Jeremy's father might have been more successful in getting his son to play if, instead of pushing him to make friends, he had offered to color along with Jeremy and Emily. His participation might have given his shy son just the boldness he needed to join in.

Luckily Emily is the kind of child who can, even at this age, ease the transition from aloneness to parallel togetherness. Jeremy, a little younger than she, will probably feel better about being with her if he starts coloring by himself and later realizes he's doing it with someone else.

Your Child/Your Role

HAS YOUR CHILD EVER:

• Thrown a tantrum when asked to play with another child?

• Remained doggedly alone, even when the teacher or counselor has managed to get all the other toddlers singing or playing in a group?

• Mimicked the actions, words, and gestures of another child as though he were looking in a mirror instead of at a potential playmate?

How You Can Encourage Appropriate Social Skills

The ability to follow rules and participate in group activities with a sense of enthusiasm and fun are the avenues by which a parallel player will one day learn to give and take with another child. But until he has managed to "do his own thing" while someone else does *his* thing beside him, he will not understand the necessary split between himself and everyone else in the world. In order to become a friend, in the adult sense, we must first accomplish the solo act. It's like the distinction between being able to play a piano concerto with an orchestra and being able to improvise as part of an interlocking harmonic and rhythmic unit in a jazz combo.

Parents may have trouble with this issue in childhood friendship because adults tend to enjoy having another person around—even a stranger—to communicate with. It's hard for some grown-ups to sit in a room concentrating on their own thoughts when they can have a pleasant conversation with the person beside them. Not so for a toddler.

The more you can appreciate your child's ability to play *beside* another child, and the more opportunities you give him to do this, the sooner he will master sharing and interacting.

Stay with your child emotionally and be supportive, but be firm when you have to be, guiding him back to a group when he's recalcitrant, or reminding him of how badly he feels when other children won't share with him.

Suppose your Strong-Willed three-year-old is having trouble with playdates and is stubbornly refusing to share toys. Maybe his playdates are just too long for him. If he's being asked to do something that hard for him, you should shorten the time he's required to do it. If he feels you're responding to his needs, he may be inclined to do the same with a friend.

You may also need to intervene more and check up on

the progress of your child's play. You can show empathy by listening to both sides, and set limits by cutting in before the bad feelings escalate and the relationship is beyond repair. Without being intrusive, you can subtly switch the children's activity, maybe getting them involved in a less competitive game or asking them to help you with an easy chore. Be sure to *praise* your child when he does share or show consideration for a friend. Emphasize the behavior he's just mastered rather than the fact that he did it well. Stay away from the epithets "good boy" or "good girl," which imply that you're judging your child on moral fiber rather than on something he or she accomplished.

If he continues to struggle through every playdate, you might give some serious thought to other possible stresses in his life right now. Is he grappling with sibling rivalry, a divorce, a new spouse, a new house, a new day-care provider? Any of these stresses may impair his burgeoning social skills.

If your child is struggling, try to spend about twenty to thirty minutes with him most days, using your Social Skills Play Kit so that he can really begin to express himself. Allow him to manipulate the toys to tell you whatever story he wishes. Use the photos of his friends to elicit his feelings about why they seem to be happy, sad, or confused. If he's hesitant, draw him out with a few pointed questions, but be careful not to put your own fix on his feelings. (You may need to recruit your partner, a grandparent, or a sitter to be with your other children in the house while you spend time with the child who needs help.)

Getting your child together with another child at this stage is tricky business. You need to tread a fine line between giving understanding and empathy and setting limits and controls. But the more you appreciate his feelings in the situation, the more competent he will feel in each subsequent interaction.

LEARNING TO NEGOTIATE:
"I will lend you my bear
for as long as I can hold my breath
if you give me that bracelet forever."

Abigail, a Strong-Willed Thinker of three, was in day care with Nancy, a Fragile Flower who was also very creative, a Thinker in her own right. Mrs. Loman, the teacher, helped the children set up tables around the room so that they could have tea parties with their toy tea sets and stuffed animals. As they were setting up their table, Abigail noticed Nancy's name bracelet. She started tugging at it, and it came right off.

"Give it back!" Nancy screamed. She started crying so hard that Mrs. Loman came over to see what was wrong.

"Abby," Mrs. Loman said, "give Nancy her bracelet."

Abigail made a face. "No!"

"Nancy, would you let Abby wear it until playground time?"

Nancy shook her head emphatically. "No!"

"How about if Abby lets you wear something of hers?" Mrs. Loman suggested. "What would you like to lend, Abby? We can make this a lending party."

Abby thought for a second and then reluctantly approached Nancy. "I will lend you my bear for as long as I can hold my breath if you will give me your bracelet forever."

Nancy looked dubious, and Mrs. Loman quickly said, "That's a good idea, except you can't keep the bracelet forever."

So Abigail lent Nancy her bear, held her breath, and when she finally expelled the air, she returned the bracelet and took back her bear.

What's Really Going On?

Abigail sees something she wants; she takes it. Nancy wants to keep a possession that's hers; she defends it. The interchange between the girls seems aggressive to an adult eye, but in reality this is a promising preparation for the bartering we see in five-to-seven-year-olds. In the next stage of development, negotiating the exchange of one thing for another is an important part of friendship.

Abigail, when convinced that she must give something up for the friendship, picks what an adult would consider an impossible choice. But it makes perfect sense to her and Nancy. The injustice of lending the bear for as long as she can hold her breath (about twenty seconds, tops!) so that she can have the bracelet forever never strikes the girls as wrong. What do they know about forever—or about twenty seconds, for that matter?

The teacher may feel frustrated by the girls' behavior, but she is right not to criticize the girls or take complete control. At least she starts the ball rolling in terms of negotiating. And when Abby makes her unreasonable suggestion, Mrs. Loman quickly turns it around so that it will work to settle the situation.

Mrs. Loman will also want to discuss this incident with Nancy's and Abigail's parents. If your child is in day care and you have heard reports from the teacher or caregiver that your child is having particular problems in one or several areas, it's a good idea to come in and observe the behavior yourself after a consultation with the adult in charge. Together you, your partner, and the day-care provider should come up with a cohesive approach. For example, the next time this occurs, the teacher might ask the children directly for ideas on how to solve the sharing problem. They may come up with some very unusual solutions, but by all means let them try different ways of negotiating, which you can fine-tune as Mrs. Loman did. In the process you and the day-care provider may learn something interesting about the give-and-take process!

When you aren't able to be with your child all day, it's

important to learn whether she's only having trouble in the day-care setting or if she also has problems negotiating with her friends at home. If she is, you can ask her day-care provider to give her lots of opportunity for give-and-take play with several different children each day. You can follow up at home with weekend playgroups or one-on-one dates. You should certainly make an appointment to go back and observe in the day-care center after your child has had a sufficient period of time to work on these skills.

Your Child/Your Role

HAS YOUR CHILD EVER:

* Hooked you into lengthy negotiation—a glass of water, another story, a hug and kiss—in order to delay bedtime?
* Offered another child a very valuable item (your watch or ring, for example) in exchange for some "found" object, such as a rock or a flower?
* Had a wonderful time playing tug-of-war over a toy, until the other child "won"?

How You Can Encourage
Appropriate Social Skills

One of the most important things to remember about your child's growing ability to be a friend is that eventually he will have to make his own decisions, fight his own battles, and rack up his own successes. If you interfere too much in the natural give-and-take process, he will always be looking for your approval instead of thinking for himself.

With infants and toddlers, however, sometimes you have to step in, because they aren't yet ready to handle advanced negotiations. They are too egocentric to function efficiently when friction starts with another egocentric pal. They have no perspective on another child's wants and needs—all they know is that what they see belongs to them.

For this reason you have to be the go-between. This doesn't mean you should do all the negotiating, but you can teach rudimentary bartering skills as you guide your young child in social situations, much as Abigail's teacher did.

A very important part of growth is learning to deal with manageable disappointments. They are not pleasant, but the earlier we learn to handle them, the more successful we'll be at letting go of our anger, forgiving our friends, and moving on. You can start teaching your child to deal with inevitable disappointments if you keep them well balanced. In other words, your child should not be overwhelmed by his losses, nor should he be completely protected from them. As time goes by, he'll be able to challenge himself by taking certain risks with friends, even if the outcome isn't quite what he wanted.

Abigail and Nancy's teacher was able to help them through a difficult negotiation. But let's assume that both Abigail and Nancy were two-year-old Naysayers, a very common social style at this age. And suppose Mrs. Loman was a chronic Worrier who got even more concerned when she perceived that a battle was about to erupt over the bracelet. The negativity between the children could spill over into the teacher's reaction—and all three might eventually be screaming at each other. In this type of situation a good "fit" is needed among all parties—if the kids are being unreasonable, the adults have to become more mellow.

In our case above, Mrs. Loman knew the children's social styles and acted accordingly. She didn't let the argument get to the point of tantrums, but instead tried to modulate the girls' actions and feelings, putting into words concepts that the girls weren't able to express themselves. She never insisted that either child think about how her playmate felt in this situation, because frankly neither child cared!

The teacher was successful because she downplayed the aggressive behavior, didn't allow it to escalate, and offered a pathway toward a solution. Older children in this age group, such as Abigail and Nancy, can usually solve their own disputes with just a little adult guidance.

One excellent method of working with your older toddler on negotiation skills is to practice at home with a "toy exchange." Use the color-coded toys from your Social Skills Play Kit. You role-play another child taking a toy away and encourage your child to protest. You can even stage a mock argument, but remind your child that he is not allowed to get physical. When it's clear that the argument isn't getting resolved, you produce a second toy and make a swap with your child. Then allow him to be the negotiator by letting him offer the swap.

Children are naturally good bargainers—aren't you amazed at how this small, unsophisticated individual wins many negotiations with you and your partner over bedtime, meals, treats, and gifts? If you can maintain your own sense of fairness and not always take your child's side in a difficult encounter with a playmate, he will start to model his behavior on yours. In this way he can learn a good balance between relinquishing his rights and demanding that he win every time.

WARNING SIGNS THAT YOUR CHILD MIGHT NEED HELP

Although all children will have problems at certain times with all of the developmental issues pertinent to this age group, they shouldn't be having trouble all the time. If they are, consult Chapter Nine, "Children Who Can't Reach Out."

In addition, ask yourself the following questions about your child. If the answer to several of the items is affirmative *on a regular basis*, your child may need professional help. Does your child

- Have tantrums at any new experience—and refuse to be consoled?
- Always seem miserable during and after any kind of confrontation over possessions?
- Never get involved in another activity after you leave him with another caregiver?
- Never engage in parallel play, but instead seeks a corner to "do her own thing" or runs over everyone else's play space?

With the information you now have about your child's early socialization from eighteen months to three years, you can assist and encourage the best friendship skills for this age and pave the way for the more developed relationships that will come next.

5

FRIENDSHIP AMONG CHILDREN AGES THREE TO FIVE

Four-year-old Clarissa was sitting in the backseat of her mother's car with her best friend, Kate. "Mommy," she yelled, "stop the car! You'll hit the big, brown poopie mountain! Look!"

"We'll drown in pee!" Kate chimed in.

Clarissa's mother took a breath and shrugged. "I think we're safe. This car can get through anything. I'll turn on the windshield wipers just to be sure." She knew she had to handle their bathroom language with humor. Otherwise it would go on all afternoon. "There," she said, turning the wipers on and off, "it's all gone."

Roger's father was working in the garden when he heard a noise from upstairs. He looked up to see three-year-old Roger and his pal, Max, squirting glue bottles out the window.

"What in the name of . . . ! What are you boys doing?"

There were whoops and giggles, then silence.

"I'm coming up to take those away from you," Roger's father declared. He didn't know what had gotten into his son. Just a few months ago Roger had been a clingy child who never misbehaved.

Lydia and Thomas, both four and a half, ran merrily around the yard, chased by Lydia's golden retriever. "I want to brush his coat," Lydia said, grabbing the dog's collar.

"Me too," Thomas agreed.

"I'll go first and brush his head, and you go next. You can do his tail," Lydia declared.

Lydia's mother was astounded. Her daughter had never been so unselfish, particularly when it came to spending time with the dog. Lydia, taking turns! Maybe she was growing up.

WHAT MAKES PARENTS ANXIOUS?

This period in a child's life is an exhilarating—sometimes overwhelming—time for parents. Your toddler has turned into a child: She has really mastered speech and movement and is now quite literally all over the place. The years from three to five, filled with exuberant, rambunctious behavior and "bathroom" talk, can make you wonder what you thought was wrong with the Terrible Twos, where no was the worst word out of your child's mouth. You always knew where to look for your toddler because separating was too painful for her—but now where is she when you call?

It was easy to be forgiving with a two-year-old. You made allowances for lack of skills in so many areas—incorrect language, lack of success in toileting, and a complete ignorance of social graces (let alone table manners!).

But we all tend to expect more of a three-year-old. She is usually out in the world on a regular basis, dealing with different friends and authority figures. We are often unreasonably disappointed in her for not abandoning all her babyish habits, and in fact for picking up some new ones. Parents of three-to-five-year-olds can find their tempers short when confronted with the mischief that bubbles up in their irrepressible children.

HOW YOUR CHILD GROWS SOCIALLY
FROM THREE TO FIVE

As toddlerhood ends, a sense of self begins to emerge. This may be the first time you have a good idea of your child's real social style and blend. A whining two-year-old who seemed to be a Strong-Willed Child and Naysayer may emerge as a sparkling Performer tempered by the good nature of an Adapter.

Your child's uninhibited behavior at this point is a necessary part of his development, and essential to good friendship skills later on. Erik Erikson, one of the leading figures in the field of psychoanalysis and author of the classic book *Childhood and Society*, described parent-child interactions as revolving around "initiative versus guilt" at this age. Your three-to-five-year-old wants to take as much initiative as possible in each of his endeavors. And this is wonderful! It shouldn't be squelched, no matter how hard it is for you to tolerate his explosion of energy and occasional floundering.

WHAT ISSUES ARE PARAMOUNT
FOR YOUR CHILD RIGHT NOW?

The main friendship issues for this age group are:

- The lessening of separation anxiety
- The development of a rambunctious sense of fun
- The use of "bad" language for power and expressiveness
- The beginning of cooperation and sharing—taking turns

Children in the three-to-five-year-old age group are just beginning to *emerge from their separation anxiety*. It may startle you to see the same child who used to cry each morning when you left him suddenly start to run down the block away from you in order to get to the sitter faster. He's not abandoning you—or his need for you—by any means; rather he now has a very focused energy to get on with the next activity. And children of this age like to initiate those activities all by themselves.

In addition they don't just play; they are suffused with a *rambunctious sense of fun.* This is true whether they are dealing with a pal or a parent. Sometimes the volatile quality of their interactions may seem antisocial to you—in fact it's just a celebration of being "me," which couldn't exist at a younger stage because there wasn't much of a "me" there. The wild play that may sometimes seem out of control is a necessary step in learning good friendship skills—you certainly don't have to encourage your three-to-five to have more enthusiasm and fun!

Part of the fun is using language, which now serves as a means of wielding power. The *use of bathroom talk* that will dismay the most unflappable parent is really a combination of two elements. The first, of course, is your child's more developed speech and vocabulary and an almost obsessive need to talk, talk, talk—about something or nothing.

The second is that there may be a beginning awareness of early feelings of sexuality, which in his mind is intricately linked with the processes of elimination (what his body produces from that general anatomical area).

Bathroom talk may be one way for the three-to-five-year-old to work off his or her sexual energies. Your best defense is a good sense of humor, which will lessen your child's guilt when you start setting inevitable limits about what he may say and when he may say it.

The wild play is frequently tempered by your child's new facility with *taking turns.* No longer need you be concerned that your child will never make it out of the parallel-play stage. Now not only does she choose to participate actively with other children, she can also give up a possession every once in a while and start to share.

THE LESSENING OF SEPARATION ANXIETY:
"That's okay, Mommy—you can go away."

It was Penny's first nursery-school interview, and her mother was concerned about her three-and-a-half-year-old Fragile Flower. She knew that at some point she'd be asked to leave Penny alone with the school's director, and she didn't like the idea of her daughter being put on the spot.

After Penny's mother and the director of the school had talked at some length while Penny played with blocks in the corner, the door of the office opened, and another child was ushered in, a timid-looking girl named Heather. The director said to Penny's mother, "Why don't you let the three of us play together now?"

When Penny's mom hesitated, Penny got up, took her mother by the hand, and led her to the door. "That's okay, Mommy. I'd like to stay here with Heather. You can go away."

What's Really Going On?

Penny is becoming a self-starter, or that's what we'd call her in later life. If only we all could retain the ambition and eager assertiveness of the three-to-five-year-old stage! Penny doesn't know the other child at all, but she's bored by hearing two grown-ups talking, and she is ready to play. By the time Penny is eight, she will make a distinction between playing with just any child and playing with someone she knows and likes. For now she is just interested in someone to help her achieve her goal—setting up those blocks.

Only a few short months ago it would have been difficult,

if not impossible, for Penny's mother to leave her with a strange child and a strange adult. At two Penny needed her mother as a buffer to accomplish smooth transitions from one experience to the next. Now it seems that Penny's not so fragile after all. Her real personality—separate from that of her parents—is emerging as she comes into contact with the world. Some new situations will be more difficult than others of course. If Heather were a Strong-Willed Child or had arrived at the interview in a terrible mood or if the director were an authoritarian figure and had dominated the meeting of the two children, Penny might have gotten scared and whiny. But in this comfortable setting her new, confident self shines.

She's also not hampered by a mother who suddenly finds herself experiencing her own brand of separation anxiety. If her mother had acted anxious about leaving, Penny might have picked up on that fearfulness and become clingy in response. It is perfectly natural to feel some pangs when your child starts moving away from you—but with practice you can keep your emotions under control.

Your Child/Your Role

HAS YOUR CHILD EVER:

- Run away from you in a crowd?
- Told you he'd rather spend the day with his friend or his friend's parent than with you?
- Abandoned his love object—the blanket or stuffed animal he's never without—in a public place?

Children show their independence at this stage in ways that are not always comfortable for their parents. If your previously introverted Shy Child or Naysayer is off meeting new friends in the playground, he may simply forget you're there. Even if he knows the rules about staying close to you in public places, if he sees something he considers fascinating, he may scoot away.

Your paramount concern, of course, is your child's safety. Your secondary concern is that he begin to learn how to manage his newfound ambition to conquer the universe. He can't understand what might really happen if he wandered off into the great big world, so it's up to you to place comfortable boundaries on his new freedom without squelching his courage to explore. Setting appropriate limits right now is extremely important for your child, and this can be accomplished in a firm but compassionate way. Clamping down hard and threatening discipline is usually ineffective with a child at this age.

The promise of a special event with another person may override your son or daughter's usual desire to be with you and may even dispel the need for any transitional love object. When he's riveted in the moment, he doesn't need his security blanket or teddy bear—and although he still needs you, he may be able to do without you for short periods of time, even though he never could before.

How You Can Encourage Appropriate Social Skills

The social skills you want to develop at this age involve leadership and initiative. If you can spur him to start making small choices on his own, he will be better equipped, as he grows, to lead himself through challenging events and to have the facility to lead others.

Don't worry too much about your child lacking empathy when he leaves you with apparent ease—he'll develop consideration for your feelings later on. Even if you feel slightly wounded when he skips merrily away, it's more important right now that you not make him feel guilty about his ability to part from you. If *you* are having some separation anxiety, you might talk it over with your partner or get some better perspective on it from other parents who have already gone through this stage.

One important social issue that you can begin to work on is getting your child to follow rules and maintain group activities. You must set limits for him so that his independence doesn't get completely out of hand. For example, if his seven-year-old sister is allowed to ride her bike all the way around the block, he may be told that he can do it with her, but *only* if they stay together at all times.

You can help to prepare your preschooler for any event by practicing with your Social Skills Play Kit, outlined in Chapter Four. Your dollhouse figurines will represent your child and his older brother or sister. Have him place the figures on toy cars (which will represent the bikes) and move them around the house on your cardboard sidewalk.

If he's having trouble staying within the boundaries you've set, you might want to try reversing roles. You be the four-year-old and let your child tell you what to do on the way to the playground. When you purposely run ahead or refuse to stop when he calls you, have him reprimand you. Playing parent will be fun for him and will also allow him to internalize the rules more quickly.

If he's still breaking the rules after a lot of practice, he'll have to walk right beside you. In order to help him work on this problem with boundaries, go back and use the dollhouse in the Social Skills Play Kit together.

You may wish to increase the responsibilities of your three-to-five-year-old gradually as she gets more accomplished in following instructions. If you live in a small town or suburb, she could be allowed to walk to the next-door neighbor's to borrow an egg; if you live in an apartment house in a city, she might be allowed to do the same as you watch her from your open door.

It's important to help your child fit his newfound freedom into a context he can share with other children and adults. Right now he's exploring and wants to feel like the first person on the moon. But he is also ready to be shown that others will want to colonize the same areas.

BAD LANGUAGE AS AN EXPRESSION OF POWER:
"We want penis-butter sandwiches!"

Jeffrey, an Adapter and a Team Player, was upstairs with his friend, Walter, also a Team Player, who tended to be a Strong-Willed Child when he was under any stress. It was the holiday season, and Jeffrey's parents had asked Walter's parents to bring Walter along to their party. The boys could play upstairs while the adults mingled.

Halfway through the rather posh event the two boys appeared together on the landing and looked down at the murmuring grown-ups standing with their drinks and hors d'oeuvres.

"We want PENIS-BUTTER SANDWICHES!" the two kids yelled in unison. Everyone looked up as the boys chanted, "Penis-butter!" over and over.

What's Really Going On?

Jeffrey and Walter know that they can stop a whole party dead in its tracks thanks to the wonderful words they now have at their disposal. What incredible power they have! They can draw all the attention from the adult activity just by using language as a tool.

The words themselves are deliciously tantalizing to use. Why is this? Along with a child's awareness of himself as a whole person comes his pride in his own gender, and consequently his friends' gender.

His new mastery of language allows him to know the words for body parts, make jokes, and repeat himself again and again to reinforce what he knows (and what you will hear, *ad infinitum*!). He is proud not only of what he's describing but also of the fact that he is able to describe it. Jeffrey's pun is pretty good word-play for a four-year-old.

The idea of gender identity and sex differentiation is important now as children ally themselves with their same-sex parent and with friends who are built just like them. A child of three or four is also fascinated by the products of his body—urine and excrement—which happen to come out of him from "down there." Even though grown-ups don't like to talk about these things, three-to-five-year-olds do! And it is hard to convince children of this age that privacy in relation to bathroom activities, nudity, or sexual matters is socially desirable.

Your three-to-five-year-old not only talks better than she used to, she can also move much more efficiently than she did a year ago. She is delighted with her improved physical agility—it's fun to climb, jump, run, and fall—and she is fascinated with the housing of her body. She wants to explore and then describe all the various nooks and crannies she can find. She may be interested in seeing or touching her own and her friends' genitals—and this interest may get more avid when your child is about five or six.

Your Child/Your Role

HAS YOUR CHILD EVER:

• Screamed "dirty" words with his friend in public, or in the presence of a grandparent or teacher, after you've told him not to?

- Substituted "bathroom words" for real words when describing an event or talking in a completely different context?

If you never know what's going to come out of your child's mouth, you may feel yourself to be on tenterhooks whenever you go anywhere. It is hard to keep a sense of humor when your child is in the midst of a nursery-school interview, or starting a new playgroup, or meeting one of your business colleagues, and he suddenly starts swearing like a trooper.

Both introverted and extroverted children seem to be equally unpredictable at this age when it comes to language. It may, however, be easier to encourage a Thinker, a Shy Child, or an Adapter to go along with your word restrictions.

How You Can Encourage the Appropriate Social Skills

The social skills you want to encourage now are following rules, maintaining group activities, and having some empathy and consideration for others. You don't want to hear this language all the time, so it's important to teach your child when it's okay to "swear" and when it's too disruptive. In a playgroup, for example, all games stop when someone yells, "Caca doody!" The other kids laugh, the teacher or parent gets upset, and the train of thought and activity is broken. At the dinner table, when people are eating or trying to have a conversation about their daily events, this kind of talk is offensive.

You have to get across the fact that even though you know that this topic and these words are of enormous interest to your child and his friends, the rest of the world either doesn't care or is repelled by it. Without hitting your point home too aggressively—which can bring on an increase in this kind of language—give your child some easy guidelines to follow.

If this is a particular problem for your child, you could declare one ten-minute period before bed as "dirty-word time." Or if dinnertime is what sets off a stream of expletives, you could ask your child to please leave the table and go to his room to say all the words he wants. He may not come back until they are all out of his system. This will encourage his sense of empathy for his family—he has to understand that others do not want to hear him talk this way at the table.

Children in this age group are experiencing some very important feelings of power and usefulness. This is why, however annoying the language and behavior may be to you, it's best not to disapprove too strongly. A child who is restricted completely from using this language will begin to think that the words and what they mean are "bad" and may consequently start to feel bad about himself in relation to his emerging sexuality.

DEVELOPMENT OF A RAMBUNCTIOUS SENSE OF FUN:
"I wasn't going to sell all of Mommy's clothes, just enough."

Daniel and Cal, both nearly five, were Thinkers, but Daniel had a lot of Performer in him, while Cal was more of a Follower. Daniel's parents had just held a yard sale, and they were putting some things away that hadn't been sold. Looking out the window at the boys, Daniel's father noticed that they had set up their little picnic table and chairs in the yard and had some fabric lying on the table. What was that stuff, he wondered, and started out to check. But as he passed his bedroom, he noticed that his wife's dresser was a mess—every drawer had been pulled out, and there were socks, shirts, sweaters, and underwear all over the floor.

When he arrived at the corner, to his horror he saw Daniel stopping several passersby asking if they would like to "buy" something at their yard sale. He raced to them just in time to stop some woman from shelling out five dollars for his wife's new lamb's-wool sweater.

"We're playing store, Daddy!" Daniel announced joyfully.

"You can't do this, boys!" he said.

But he just couldn't get angry when he looked at their disappointed faces. "Mommy would be really cold without her clothes," he said firmly.

"We're not going to sell all of them," Cal explained. "Just the ones she doesn't need."

What's Really Going On?

Daniel and Cal, like most children their age, revel in fantasy play. The playacting they enjoy (whether it's playing store or dressup or fireman or astronaut) feels absolutely real to them. The boys have a plan, they have a method of execution, they cooperate in order to put the plan into effect, and they get a good result from it (a potential sale). And they are having a wonderful time until Dad suddenly stops them. His adult, rational objections don't make sense to them at all.

You may say that Daniel and Cal are "old enough" to understand that if they got rid of Daniel's mother's clothes, she wouldn't have any. You might think that riffling through Daniel's mother's drawers and hailing passersby to harangue them for money is antisocial behavior. On the contrary. For the three-to-five-year-old, this is a positive indication that they are developing the kind of ingenious initiative that will propel them through life. Their excitement about their store and its goods, their sales techniques, and their ability to motivate "buyers," take precedence over their concern for

Mommy's comfort and what it would mean to replace her clothes.

The boys are sorting out their own interests and abilities by trying on different roles. By taking different parts in their imaginative scenario—the storekeeper, the cashier, the salesman—Mark and Cal are discovering new skills and new facets of themselves.

This is not to say that it's perfectly okay to let them go ahead and let their play run its course. It's fine to allow rambunctious behavior, but only to a point. The children have to be given limits even if they don't like them.

Your Child/Your Role

HAS YOUR CHILD EVER:

- Purposely hidden with a friend and refused to come out when you call?
- Cut his friend's hair or a piece of her clothing?
- Injured a friend with a homemade weapon?

It's often hard for the three-to-five to know how elastic those boundaries might be. He is having so much fun, he may be completely abandoned in his mischief making, and a pal's hair or clothing may be shredded in the process. Extroverts, particularly, are always moving, and they aren't careful about who may be in their way. You may be tempted to accuse your Strong-Willed Child, Performer, or Team Player of being thoughtless and mean when he turns the garden hose on his friend or swings a toy on a string until it hits his pal in the face, but this is not deliberately hurtful behavior. His goal right now is to hit his target, and that target happens to be his friend. The friend may accept this as part of their play and, unless he's really injured, will probably laugh and enjoy it.

Introverts tend to be less physically forceful in their rambunctious play. But your Shy Child, Thinker or Fragile Flower may surprise you. Two quiet children may disappear on an "adventure" in a closet for fifteen minutes and refuse to respond to calls, causing their parent to experience acute heart palpitations.

How You Can Encourage
Appropriate Social Skills

Following rules is the skill you really *want* to encourage—but you may feel you are getting nowhere if you talk about it too much. Your three-to-five-year-old may agree to all of your rules and then immediately break them. He will act chagrined and promise he will never do such a thing again, only to repeat the infraction or do something else that's prohibited.

When a parent makes too big a distinction between "right" and "wrong" behavior at this age, he may gradually wear down his child's sense of enthusiasm and fun by making him feel guilty. If a child is always second-guessing himself about what he should or shouldn't do, he may lose all confidence and become withdrawn—or he may act out in rebellion.

It is true that you are no longer dealing with a two-year-old who can't be expected to "know better." The toddler who runs off in a crowd isn't "thinking" about whether this is appropriate behavior. The three-to-five-year-old, on the other hand, knows it's wrong, but forgets because something else becomes more important to him than the rule.

Instead of emphasizing the necessity for rules and regulations, try to encourage his willingness and ability to participate in group activities. If you can tell him how eager you are to hear his plans for play, he may start reporting to you before he takes all your clothes out of the drawer or disembowels the clock. This puts the burden on you to come up with some alternatives that will be equally appealing to him, but you may forestall some real destruction.

You can also encourage your child's sense of empathy and consideration. Although a child of this age is too young to be able to take another person's perspective, you can role-play to show him how his actions affect his friends and his parents.

Using the puppets or dollhouse dolls from your Social Skills Play Kit, you can make it clear that it's okay to have fun so long as it doesn't hurt anyone else.

You can schedule fun—supervised events such as cookie baking and car washing—to channel rambunctious energy into something useful. Going back to our earlier example, Daniel and Cal could be encouraged to have their own yard sale several days later where they could sell paper airplanes they'd constructed or some old toys or books. They could set up a lemonade stand, or sell seashells they've gathered at the beach. Any activity that gets the children to rechannel their creative initiative would be beneficial.

TAKING TURNS:
*"I'll ride the car first,
then you, and then me again, okay?"*

Jan, a Boss who could also be a Performer, always gravitated toward the riding toys at preschool. When a parent donated a special battery-powered car to the school, Jan was quicker than any other four-year-old to grab it.

Ms. Arica, the teacher, tried to persuade Jan to share, but when the child started whining and complaining, Ms. Arica took the car and put it in the back room for the rest of the day.

The next morning the car was put out again, and Jan hopped into it. Jan's friend Lisa, a five-year-old Fragile

Flower/Thinker, came over, and Ms. Arica overheard the girls talking.

"You can't ride in my car, it's too special," Jan said, touching it protectively.

"I just want to see what it's like. Please can I?"

Jan got in the car and steered it around the yard.

"I never saw one of those cars before," Lisa said. "And I probably never will again," she added pitifully.

Jan bit her lip and furrowed her eyebrows. "If you *really* want to ride," she said, "I get to go first, then you, then me again. Okay?"

"Okay," Lisa said agreeably.

What's Really Going On?

Jan is having problems with the idea of sharing her most prized possession. She recalls that her teacher has already put the car away once for her lack of willingness to participate with others, so she knows she might jeopardize her own chances to ride the car if she continued this behavior with Lisa. But Jan is an extrovert, so she's able to give a little so long as she can remain in control.

Lisa succeeds in this situation by using her head. Because of her particular social style, she wouldn't just run over and try to muscle the car away from Jan. She uses feelings to influence her friend, and succeeds in getting what she wants.

But, as a Boss, Jan is still in control. She has set up the "deal" so that she gets the first and the last turn—always one more turn than her friend will have.

Had the roles been reversed and had Jan been a Shy Child and Lisa a Boss, the interchange might have been totally different. Jan might have immediately given up her car when intimidated and been unable to get it back, even if she whined and complained. Neither girl would have ended up happy, and this might have soured their relationship.

The girls are learning to accommodate their needs with those of another person. They couldn't have done this a year ago. During the toddler years, relationships with other children are in part substitutes for the intense dealings that children have with their parents. These early "friendships" are extremely useful because they allow kids to separate comfortably from Mommy and Daddy.

But during the three-to-five stage your child's friendships are beginning to take on meaning in and of themselves—you don't figure into them. For this reason it's wise to allow your child the conflicts she will inevitably have as she learns how to bargain in her relationships.

It is very difficult to predict if and when your child will agree to take turns. If your child is at preschool during the day and you've had reports from the teacher that she's having difficulty sharing, you should make it a point to observe the class, consult with the teacher about how to handle the problem, and come back for a second visit after a suitable period of time has passed. On weekends notice how your child handles sharing with her friends while a parent is around.

Different sets of three-to-five-year-olds will have different ways of sharing and cooperating with each other. As with Jan and Lisa, it was better for the teacher to stay uninvolved.

Some days your child will have terrific playtimes, and some days it may seem that all you do is break up fights. On the bad days remember that this is the first time your son or daughter has had the social skills to use and the inclination to use them.

Your Child/Your Role

HAS YOUR CHILD EVER:

- Agreed to play a game and then changed all the rules to suit himself?

- Said that he would take turns on a piece of playground equipment and then kept the other children hanging as he took one turn after another?
- Cooperated in a group activity and then sulked afterward because he didn't have enough "fun"?

Although a child of this age knows that other people have feelings, he looks at this "other" in a very egocentric way.

He may change all the rules to certain games, assuming that everyone wants to play it the way he does. He may agree to put his own interests aside for the good of the group and play the game the way the caregiver or teacher sets it up, and then later complain that "it's no good that way."

He may know that his friend is afraid of going down the slide, but he may still insist that they play on the slide together. This is an activity he likes and wants to share—and he can't understand why his friend doesn't like it just as much as he does.

His confusion between his own desires and someone else's comes to a head when the other child bursts out crying. Even though he doesn't know what's wrong, he feels sorry that his pal is upset and tries to comfort him. He does have a burgeoning sense of empathy, which will really come to the fore in the next few years. But a three-to-five-year-old's version of empathy doesn't often allow him to see the problem from anyone else's perspective. Once his friend's tears are dried, he'll once again try to coax him into going down that slide.

How You Can Encourage Appropriate Social Skills

Learning to share and take turns is a long, slow process, and even many adults have trouble with these skills!

You can probably do the most active work with your

child on nonverbal rapport. This is one area where you can model behavior yourself, or role-play imaginary scenarios with the figurines or hand puppets from your Social Skills Play Kit. When you take your child to the playground, you can point out kids his age who are cooperating successfully by relying on one another without words—maybe two who are building a sand castle or a block structure together. You can also remind him of times where he has succeeded on his own with sharing. Focus on what he does right. The more positive reinforcement he can get, the more he'll repeat the behavior.

Encourage your child's participation in a group, which may be somewhat easier at this age than a one-on-one play-date. One of the reasons children of this age do begin to share and cooperate with others is that their peer group has taken on greater importance for them. No longer does the three-to-five-year-old rely solely on parental influence; now she can rally the rudimentary support of several friends her own age.

Group activities are held together when everyone is doing her part. If your child's preschool teacher organizes a circle of Ring Around the Rosy or another singing or clapping game, your child will get the idea that the whole depends on the integrity of its parts. If everyone is singing and clapping, she may too. Once she's used to cooperating in a group, she will be more attuned to sharing during play with just one friend.

WARNING SIGNS THAT YOUR CHILD MIGHT NEED HELP

Many parents get anxious about whether their child is progressing emotionally at the same level as other children they know. Remember that development of friendship skills comes more slowly to some than to others. Don't be concerned if your child occasionally has trouble with the issues

pertinent to this age group. If he is having problems frequently, however, consult Chapter Nine, "Children Who
Can't Reach Out."

In addition ask yourself the following questions about
your child. If the answer to several of the items is affirmative
on a regular basis, your child may need professional help:

- Is it still very difficult, even at five years old, for your
child to separate from you? Does she remain very upset long
after you've gone?
- Does he often run away from you? Does he ever hide
from you so that you can't find him?
- Has your child ever really injured another child in
the course of play? Does he seem unaware of his strength?
- Is she always intimidated by boisterous play with
other children?
- Will she never take turns?
- Does he always relinquish his turn when another
child pushes ahead?

With the information you now have about your child's
friendships from three to five years old, you can assist and
encourage the best friendship skills for this age. You can also
breathe a sigh of relief, because your child is about to enter
a quieter, more adaptable period where he can begin to develop more complex, empathic relationships with others.

6

FRIENDSHIP AMONG CHILDREN AGES FIVE TO SEVEN

"I won't go to kindergarten, Mommy," five-and-a-half-year-old Darcy declares, "if I can't bring my Lambie and my blankie and don't have to share them with anybody else." You look at her in confusion. Just yesterday she acted so mature, so excited about the prospect of going to school. Why is she suddenly babyish and unreasonable?

"I'm not talking to anyone in the playground today," snarls six-year-old Larry. "There's no good kids in the whole school." You're taken aback. Larry is such a friendly child, he likes almost everyone he meets. You've never seen him act antisocial—yet now he seems to be at war with the world.

"You can't come in!" shrieks your seven-year-old daughter, locked in her bedroom with a girlfriend from down the block. You demand to be let in or else, and discover the two children half undressed in the bed. Swallowing hard, you fumble for a way to cover your embarrassment. You worry about all the sexual behaviors that this might imply. How are you supposed to handle it?

WHAT MAKES PARENTS ANXIOUS?

It's very easy to misinterpret what's happening with your children's friendships at this stage. Your daughter may swear on Friday afternoon that the next-door neighbor is her "very best friend forever." Then at the movies the next day she looks right through her when she sees her standing next to another child. This is not pathological behavior, it's simply a different set of circumstances and a lack of practice in necessary social skills. Remember that children are always straddling several different developmental and cognitive-ability levels. They will naturally switch back and forth, sometimes with lightning speed.

Children need time—to grow into new stages, to relapse into comfortable old ones, and mostly to find their footing in each different situation that confronts them.

After an hour with her new classmates your timid kindergartener will probably be having a ball, able to give and take with new friends as a competent, social, well-adjusted individual. The six-year-old who screams at the end of play-dates because he has trouble with transitions from one activity to another will change in time into someone who can handle change with grace and ease. The children who seem obsessed with each other's bodies will evolve into independent, trusting friends who, by seven and a half, may not have much interest at all in their potential sexuality because they are now in a new stage of personal exploration, developing skills and abilities.

HOW YOUR CHILD GROWS SOCIALLY FROM FIVE TO SEVEN

Children with different social styles naturally glean different elements from this time of their lives. For the extroverts— the Team Player, the Boss, the Performer, the Strong-Willed

Child and the Adapter—the time from age five to seven is a many-course banquet. An outgoing child will delight in having new friends, new opportunities such as clubs to join and teams to play on, and so many other ways to get involved in life outside the home.

For the introverts, who cope better in a one-on-one situation—the Shy Child, the Thinker, the Follower, the Naysayer, and the Fragile Flower—this time can be difficult, though challenging, since participation in group activities and developing friendship skills are crucial to a child's unfolding personality. These children may need help being more assertive, both in entering any social situation and in sticking up for themselves once they're there. You may have to do some role-playing with a Shy Child on how to approach a group of kids in the midst of a game, for example. Or you could remind her of how successful she was the time she convinced her bossy friend that it was her turn to use the swing.

With both introverts and extroverts, expect to see behavior patterns that shift with quicksilver speed. Sometimes your inner-directed child will show off skills that seem much more appropriate for an extrovert, and vice versa. This is a time of trial and error as children feel their way into friendships, trying on skills for size and honing them in their own particular ways.

Knowing your child's blend of social styles will make you better able to help her through the rough times in friendships and cheer her on through her growth and evolution. When you know more about the conflicting issues that arise during this developmental period, you'll be better able to act effectively and not be confused or dismayed by difficult moments.

WHAT ISSUES ARE PARAMOUNT
FOR YOUR CHILD RIGHT NOW?

The main friendship issues for this age group are:

- Bartering toys or other concrete items for friendship
- Exerting or relinquishing control of a situation
- Developing empathy
- Sexuality
- Determining their own sense of right and wrong

Children in the five-to-seven-year-old age group tend to cement their friendship by *sharing possessions* and activities. Kids trade items, rather than feelings or ideas, at this time of life. Cognitively they understand the world in very concrete terms—if someone hands them a present, that spells "nice." If someone accidentally tears their drawing, that spells "mean." They cannot yet distinguish between the subtleties of behavior, which become increasingly abstract as they mature.

They also have a lot of concern about *control* in different situations, since they are now increasingly aware of other children as separate human beings with wants and needs different from their own. Now they can see that they are not "omnipotent" and that others have rights too.

This realization can be scary, because it threatens a child's place in the world. Thus the five-to-seven-year-old may do everything possible to exert control over situations ("I won't go to kindergarten if I can't bring my Lambie," and so on). A child can gradually let go of this illusion of power as he is better able to handle reality. As he tries to find the middle ground between control and letting go, however, his behavior may fluctuate. Sometimes this child may seem like the leader in a friendship; at other times he may be the follower.

Because a child in this age group has come to understand the difference between himself and another, he can begin to develop a sense of *empathy,* the ability to understand someone else's perspective and feelings. Prior to this time a child sees the world from the narrow range of his own experience. We may, of course, see a three-year-old pat a crying friend on the back and offer him a cookie, but this isn't really empathy. It's more like a personal reaction to his own feelings, as if he were taking care of himself when he was sad. By the time your child is five, however, he can *sometimes* imagine what his friend is feeling even if it's different from what he's going through himself. This allows him to take the comforting position more frequently and in a more mature manner.

From time to time you'll see changes in your child's ability to feel empathy. For example, she might offer a pal her favorite teddy bear to hold when her friend is homesick on the first day of kindergarten; or she might tell you she's going to keep the "Old Maid" for the next hand of cards because her friend never gets to win and this will make her feel better. The exercises in this chapter, "Develop Your Child's Empathy Energy," will be useful in encouraging your child's growing potential with this skill.

Sexuality between friends, expressed by going to the bathroom together, looking at each others' genitals, and discussing bodily functions, is common in many children, but some will manifest this little or not at all. Sexuality tends to upset parents more than many other issues that emerge at this stage. In addition, the attachment to the parent of the opposite sex is very strong right now.

Frequently, by age seven or eight some of these feelings of sexuality go underground. There tends to be a slackening of interest in sexuality as children get more into learning and organized group activities. However, some experts feel that children's sexual energy is always there—it's simply diverted into other pursuits, achievements, and interests until adolescence, when it blossoms!

At the same time, children are starting to develop a conscience. This stage includes the real emergence of a sense of right and wrong. Children help one another develop rules for life by mimicking what they have learned at home and testing it in the real world. The influence of different parenting styles obviously molds a child's perception of the world— of how "we" do it and how "they" do it.

A child from a family with clear-cut, strict rules may form a strong friendship with a child from a liberal, laissez-faire household, and together they may figure out ways of behaving that combine the two styles of parenting. The "free" child may do some wild, creative fantasizing about making money so that she and her friend can buy new dress-up clothes; the "strict" child may suggest that the two of them set up a sidewalk stand (with their parents' permission of course!) and sell their old toys in order to accomplish that goal.

In this way friends can help to solidify a child's burgeoning "internal policeman," who guides daily decisions. Eventually, as he grows older, this inner guiding voice will foster his very own moral worldview.

BARTERING FOR FRIENDSHIP:
"Will you be my friend if I give you . . . ?"

Henry and Pat, five-and-a-half-year-old Team Players, were playing one afternoon. Henry, who had many traits of the Strong-Willed Child, got up to use the bathroom, telling Pat to leave everything just the way it was. When Henry returned, however, Pat (something of a Thinker, with his own ideas about doing things) had appropriated all of Henry's model cars. Henry swiped at them to get them back, and Pat sulkily turned away. They swore angrily that they would never be friends again.

The next weekend Pat was playing with his superhero figurines at the pool when he noticed Henry, who'd just walked through the gate with his mother. As the mothers chatted, Pat approached his estranged friend. But Henry wouldn't even look at him.

Pat then took out his new superhero character and pressed it into Henry's hand.

"You can keep him . . . if you'll be friends again," Pat offered. Henry looked up and smiled.

What's Really Going On?

At the age of five, gift giving is a normal expression of friendship. It's the best way a child at this stage can tell another friend that he likes him and wants to be with him. Depending on your child's blend of social styles and the particular social skills he has, he may give or withhold toys in effective or less effective ways. And his effectiveness with giving and taking also depends, in great part, on his timing.

When a child has a good sense of timing, he knows *when* to assert himself, *when* to ask if he can join in an activity, *when* to go over and extend help to a friend. Good timing is one of the most crucial friendship skills as we get older because it hinges on our ability to read another person's desires accurately and make ours coincide with theirs. Sometimes if we miss the right moment, it may take longer to make up after a fight because the other person is no longer ready to hear what we have to say. It's easier for a kid with a good sense of timing who isn't so egocentric to share; it's harder for a demanding child, who may have more rigid expectations about what friends should and shouldn't do.

In the situation above, sharing possessions is a symbol

of both boys' need to reestablish good feelings. The way in which the gift was offered ("I'll give you this if you give me that") may seem crass to an adult, but in reality the superhero character is just an icebreaker. This concrete, external object acts as an extension of the boys' feelings for one another and allows Henry and Pat to focus on something outside themselves and their disagreement. The toy serves as a conduit for overcoming their estrangement. They don't have to apologize or acknowledge that they were "wrong" or made a mistake—they can save face simply by making a peace offering.

Even older children may rely on the exchange of gifts to cement a friendship. A seven-year-old Naysayer may insist that a Performer buddy take a bag of toys home after a playdate and return them exactly three days later, at their next date. Because the first child has definite leadership potential and a real need to set the rules up her way, she is very persuasive about getting her friend to do exactly as she wants. The other child, also a leader but excellent at following rules and possessing a good sense of timing, can agree to her friend's offer.

Exchanging this kind of promise about material goods shows that the girls like each other enough to want to play together again in the near future.

To return to our earlier example, if Pat had had less empathy and consideration and less willingness to interact with his friend, he might have found it much more difficult to negotiate the exchange of goods—even if he thought he'd be able to get something in return. And if Henry had been the type of child who shied away from confrontation and felt hurt when criticized, he might have had trouble meeting Pat halfway and accepting the toy as a peace offering. A hypersensitive child often can't see the goodwill behind an action if he's too busy examining the little things his friend did to hurt his feelings. Since Henry had the social skills to understand and accept Pat's solution, however, and since Pat excelled socially in passing on his sense of enthusiasm to his pal, they were able to give each other the chance to return to a better place in the friendship.

Your Child/Your Role

HAS YOUR CHILD EVER:

- Promised to invite another child to a party if he'll bring him a certain present he wants?
- Filled a friend's pockets with toys to make sure that that friend will like her?
- Ungraciously handed another child a toy saying, "Here, you can have this—I don't want it anymore"?

Whether your child is busy bartering, hoarding, or giving away his toys, he is in some sense using *things* as tools in his early friendship experiences.

If your child has fought with another over possessions— a likely occurrence at this age—the best thing to do is to hang back and not pressure him to make up. Though he may vow never to talk to his "enemy" again, the cooling-off period may take as little as twenty-four hours. It's important to let your child blow off steam by complaining to you about his friend. This is an important prelude to his wanting to make up. If you can understand how your listening helps him to work this through, you won't feel so anxious about how angry he is.

If reconciliation is taking a lot longer, however, it may be helpful to give your child the opportunity to meet and make up, perhaps on neutral turf—that is, not at either one's house. By getting together with the other child's parent, you can act as a model for the kind of friendly behavior you'd like your children to emulate.

How You Can Encourage
Appropriate Social Skills

The social skills you want to develop at this age are the abilities to solve problems and make peace. Remember that for a very young child those are sophisticated concepts. You may want to start by encouraging your child to be willing to participate in play with his friend once again. This may help him to recapture the sense of enthusiasm and fun he had with his friend. If you can encourage him to think about the good times he's had with his friend and remind him of a few other times he's made up with a pal after a fight, he may be able to find the path to peace by himself. You might remind him about the other day when you got angry at Daddy for taking your book back to the library without asking if you'd finished it, and he made up by going back and borrowing it for you again. This example could help your child in his own situation, because it's about two partners reestablishing their closeness after a break. It can also show him—without preaching or lecturing—that he's not the only one who has to resolve conflicts with people he cares about.

Remember, too, that you don't want to let your child feel that his anger was bad. It's important for him to know that anger is just like any other emotion to be expressed within the context of a close friendship, but that it can be dealt with and then allowed to dissolve. If you tell your five-to-seven-year-old that he was bad for being so mean to his pal, he may begin to feel that he's bad, period.

It is crucial that children be permitted to express their feelings—even negative ones—to each other. Only by doing this and seeing the effects of their actions will they learn what friends will and will not tolerate in the friendship. This knowledge of another person's boundaries enables them to proceed to the next, more bonded type of relationship.

Be wary of expecting a child of this age to act as you

would in a similar circumstance. If you criticize your child for trying to "buy" another's friendship with a toy, or wince when she pushes a toy on a friend and tactlessly says she's giving it away because she no longer wants it, you may undermine her good intentions. A child who's sensitive to criticism will be crushed if you break empathy this way, and even a more resilient child will lose self-esteem. Remember, your five-to-seven-year-old isn't ready to talk on an abstract level about what went wrong. Respect her way of doing things, and praise the fact that she's discovered her own way of making up. Don't worry—the other child isn't going to be hurt by your child's less-than-tactful tactics; he's at the same stage himself.

If your child has had a fight with a friend and the reconciliation isn't happening, it may be that the timing is wrong. Extroverted children may be too proud to make up quickly or may still be holding onto their anger from the hostile encounter; introverted ones may find that the loss of self-esteem in having to say "I'm sorry" is just too much to handle.

Your child may simply need to talk with you more about what happened with her friend and how bad it made her feel. Betrayal and humiliation are difficult to handle at any age, and if she can sense that you sympathize and that she has an ally in you, she may eventually be able to give or receive an apology.

If your child is holding a grudge, you might try asking your librarian to suggest some children's books that discuss holding grudges, or you can take a look at any of the recommended children's titles in the Bibliography at the end of this book. You might also play a game where you take turns making up twenty ways to say you're sorry. You can use the photos in your Social Skills Play Kit to show friends looking angry and then happy. Have your child make up scenarios in which she is able to effect a change of behavior in a friend by something she does or says.

Don't press your child to make amends because you're concerned about what the other parent will think or because you're worried that your child isn't making progress with her social skills. If she can't feel good about how she handles her friendships, she will have increasing difficulty believing that she's worthy of her friends' admiration. This could harm her abilities to make or retain close friendships in the future.

EXERTING OR RELINQUISHING CONTROL:
"You do what I say, or else!"

Kendra, age seven, is a Boss. She will emphatically tell anyone what to do and how to do it—kids, parents, and teachers. Her friend Gerry, five and a half, is pretty easygoing but tends to be a blend of a Follower and a Shy Child. He won't often take the lead and tends to back off from participating in events, even though he's awfully good at a variety of activities.

Kendra and Gerry were walking home from school when they passed a church with a high wall. Kendra dared Gerry to climb on top of it and jump off.

"I don't want to, it's too high," Gerry objected.

"You do it or else I'll tell everybody in your little baby kindergarten class that you're a scaredy-cat!" she challenged him.

Reluctantly Gerry got on the wall and took a few hesitant steps. He was just starting to feel okay about the height when he noticed that Kendra wasn't even looking at him.

"I'm doing it!" he shouted. "Are you going to try it?"

"I could if I wanted," Kendra countered. "You just better not tell anyone I didn't get up there or you'll be sorry."

What's Really Going On?

Kendra is relishing the power that comes from getting other people to do what she wants. In another few years, if she can temper these manipulative tendencies, she may become less of a Boss and more of a Strong-Willed Child, an enthusiastic leader who is determined to get her own way, but not at the expense of others. This changing of blend is apparent with every type, as children grow and mature. Who knows—with her leadership qualities, by the time Kendra is thirty-five, she might be a good candidate for president!

Gerry, in turn, needs to focus on that moment when he stopped thinking about his fears and realized he had mastered the wall—and that his tormentor wasn't even able to do what he could do! With more reliance on his strengths— his willingness to participate and follow rules and his sense of fun—he could turn from a child who lets others mold him to a kid who's a Team Player but who isn't afraid to take risks. He'll be able to rely on his excellent physical abilities to make the most of any situation—even those that are difficult for him.

Who's the leader; who's the follower? This question comes up in so many friendships at this age. The interesting thing about both introverts and extroverts is that if they can be more adaptable to others' wishes, they can shift from one role to the other, depending on whom they play with. Sometimes you can encourage your child to try out a less characteristic behavior when he is with a child whose personality is similar to his. A Thinker, for example, might have the courage to take the lead with a Shy Child, whereas he might not put himself forward with a more aggressive friend.

Your Child/Your Role

HAS YOUR CHILD EVER:

- Tried to force another child to perform a dangerous trick as a proof of friendship?
- Threatened to "tell" if another child is breaking a well-known rule?

- Come home crying after a playdate but refused to tell you what his friend did to him?
- Begun to emulate a friend's stronger or weaker behavior?

Children of this age are experts at maneuvering situations so that they can get control of them. If you have an extrovert, you've probably noticed how he can get his own way by demanding or challenging. An introvert can wield the same power, just by acting helpless and clingy and getting everyone to pay attention to her.

No matter what your child's social style, it's important that she get practice in *both* leading *and* following. If she always gravitates toward a relationship where she is the dominant force, or one in which she is the submissive one, it's a good idea for you to encourage her to switch roles. You might tell her that you and your best friend used to take turns, one being the mommy or the daddy and one being the baby, when you played together. You can even playact this way with your child, allowing her alternately to boss you around and then take instructions from you. A Simon Says game would be a perfect way to do this in a structured manner.

If you see that she's stuck in a very rigid relationship with another child who is inflexible about changing roles, it may be time for you to step in. You'll know that you should take a more active part if, say, your child seems unhappy about her playdates with this particular child and the power balance between them is always weighted in one direction. She may tip you off to the fact that she can't help herself by saying, "Amy *made* me do it. I knew it was wrong, but I couldn't help it." Or you may overhear another child bossing your child, who's sulking about the treatment she's getting but unable to change it. This is a pattern that needs to be broken, since it can be very destructive for your child to

continue in a relationship where she is constantly manipulated and can't turn things around when necessary.

In order to encourage your child to get out of her rut,
you might want to invite a new friend and his or her family
over for a meal or suggest a special outing for your child and
this new friend, such as going to a movie or a trip to the
circus. It may be easier for your child to abandon the "stuck"
friendship if he gets into a relationship with another child
where there's a healthy give-and-take. You may even find that
he is able to return to the "stuck" friendship and rebalance it
after a few months' experience in a more flexible relationship.

How You Can Encourage
Appropriate Social Skills

The social skills you want to encourage include those that will
put your child out front with a friend or a group and those
that will let your child hang back, listen, and help. If you
have a child who's always ready to take over any situation,
you'd certainly want her to continue to feel successful at
what she does best, which is leading and organizing others.
However, you also want to ensure that she isn't using her
dominating abilities to make a friend act for her—or act just
like her.

For example, if you've asked the kids to clean up after
playtime and you notice that your child is making her friend
do all the work, you can call a halt to things and give them
both specific cleaning responsibilities. You might point out
that the job gets done faster when people share the work.
Without making your child feel guilty or haranguing her
about fairness, you should be able to trigger some more coop-
erative behavior.

If your child tends to be reluctant about participating in
social events, make sure you let him know he can be proud

of his ability to show empathy, analyze situations, and act when the time is right. You also want to encourage his trust so that he can come to you and discuss whether another child is bossing him and why he's putting up with it.

Take every opportunity to make a child of this age aware of others' needs. If you brought a snack to the playground, you could ask your Shy Child to offer some crackers to another kid you recognized from his kindergarten class; if you saw a playmate trip and fall, you might ask your Strong-Willed Child to help him up. In this way you can gently stimulate different behavior over time as he plays with different children.

DEVELOPING EMPATHY:
"Don't feel bad; I'll help you!"

Elise and Mary, both just seven, were at the playground, climbing on the equipment. Elise, a blend of Performer and Team Player, was demonstrating to Mary, a Fragile Flower who was pretty adaptable, how to perform a backward somersault on the rings. Mary attempted it and fell on her wrist, breaking the skin. She started to cry.

"Oh, come on, it's not that bad," Elise said.

"It hurts."

Elise whipped her T-shirt out of her pants and quickly wiped Mary's eyes. "Come on, I'll help you. Try again—I know you can do it," she encouraged her friend.

Mary got back on the equipment and, with a push from Elise, tried unsuccessfully to spin around. She grunted and again landed hard on the ground.

Elise executed a perfect spin, then another. "Ha, ha! I can do it and you can't!" she chanted as Mary began crying again.

What's Really Going On?

Empathy in seven-year-olds is still a now-you-see-it, now-you-don't proposition. Elise is kind one minute, appearing to understand how rotten Mary feels, then smug and full of herself the next.

A child of this age can put herself in another's shoes for just so long. Then, as she becomes more involved in the situation, her own ego comes to the fore. But the more self-esteem she has, the more likely it is that she can be empathic, because she is secure enough to be able to concentrate less on her own concerns and shortcomings and more on another's perspective.

If Elise had an even higher degree of self-confidence for her age than she does, she'd be able to comfort Mary and not turn around and taunt her. If Mary had better self-esteem, she would be able to take her own shortcomings in stride. She could say, "Yeah, sometimes I'm pretty klutzy. Let me try it again." As it is, her feelings of worth aren't yet high enough to allow her to take her friend's criticism lightly, because she's so concerned with "fixing herself." This narrow focus is very common in many children of this age.

It's also hard to be empathic if you're worrying about "what's fair," a concept that comes up with all types of children at this stage. For example, if Mary had such low self-esteem that she was envious of her friend's advanced physical skills, she might have had trouble playing with Elise. If she thought it wasn't fair that someone else could do what she was incapable of doing, she might have been reluctant even to try somersaulting on the rings.

If Elise didn't have a natural sense of enthusiasm, she might have thought it wasn't fair for her to have to play with a "baby." But as the two become closer in their physical abilities and acquire the emotional maturity to become less frustrated about not being able to accomplish certain athletic goals, their empathy level with each other will rise.

Your Child/Your Role

HAS YOUR CHILD EVER:

• Thoughtfully agreed to leave you alone when you were feeling ill and then proceeded to make more noise than five kids put together?

• Played beautifully with a younger sibling for hours, then suddenly turned on him, screaming and hitting for no reason?

• Made a special tea party to welcome a friend home after a long trip, then refused to let the child use any of her toys at the party?

How You Can Encourage Appropriate Social Skills

Empathy is the major social skill that you'd like to encourage in your child at this time. But it's an elusive goal, and harder for extroverted children, who may be more set on getting their own way than their milder-mannered counterparts. So you might start by encouraging your extroverted child to wait and observe a situation instead of rushing in to join the fun.

To help your child practice taking another's perspective, you might try going to a playground with her and agreeing to be "spies," just watching interactions between other children. When you see a situation or overhear a conversation in which one child is being particularly understanding of another's problem, stop and listen together.

Say you've found a couple of seven-year-old girls playing Pick-Up Sticks, arguing over whether a stick moved or not. A typical parental tactic—and one that hardly ever works—

is to lecture your child about how she should "give in" every once in a while just to be nice, or allow a friend to be right even when she thinks she's wrong.

Instead let your child feel what it might be like to be somebody else by asking her to assume both roles, one after the other. Suggest that she first pretend to be the girl who moved the stick—what would she say and do? Now suggest that she switch roles and pretend to be the other one who wants a turn—what would she say and do? By standing outside a real situation and "rehearsing" for the actual event, your extrovert will begin to sense empathy for another.

Some experts say that empathy in children of this age correlates with the amount of time they spend with their fathers. One reason for this may be that a child perceives his mother as part of himself for the first year or so of life; the father is therefore the first "other" a child knows and so can be a powerful stimulus for getting the child to understand the feelings of the "other." Also, fathers tend to set more limits because they are usually not willing to put up with waffling, whining, or other unpleasant behaviors. Children therefore seem to learn to respect boundaries—the "separateness of the other"—from their fathers.

After enough experiences with limit-setting, children learn that they must occasionally give something up in order to remain in harmony with another person. By understanding what someone else needs in a situation, they can start to feel for the other person.

Modeling empathic behavior is a great way to teach children to see another's point of view and feel for that person's needs.

For example, one mother, who took her daughter swimming at the local pool, always helped a certain elderly lady to take her shoes off in the locker room when they were changing their clothes. The rather demanding, hypersensitive child, who often missed the subtleties of relationships, got to see her mother tending to a person who needed her, figuring out exactly what needed doing and being casually helpful, not too pushy or overly solicitous.

Months later the mother happened to look out the window and caught her daughter tending to the little girl next door, who had just fallen off her bike. She had clearly absorbed the message of empathy without being told a thing.

You certainly can and should praise a child who can take another child's perspective, even if you don't agree with that perspective. If your Fragile Flower always sticks up for the negative Naysayer, he may be "trying on" his friend's behavior by attempting to understand it. This doesn't mean he's going to acquire that pal's social style. But it may mean that he will learn some useful skills that will help him to assert himself more readily.

DEVELOPING YOUR CHILD'S EMPATHY

Here is a set of exercises that you can do with your five-to-seven-year-old child to help him develop empathy for others. You can adapt these suggestions for an older child, eliminating the fantasy and play elements and simply talking out real-life situations with him.

1. Name five things you could do for a sick friend if you couldn't talk.
2. Imagine that your friend is a color. Now think how his color would change if he'd just been punished by his parents. What are the feelings you associate with these two different colors?
3. What song could you sing to a friend who's not invited to a party that all her other friends are going to? How would you sing to her? (loud, soft, silly, etc.?)

4. List twenty things a lonely boy could do to make himself feel better.

5. Pretend you've just been stranded on a desert island with a snobby girl you don't like. Name five things you could do that would help you work together.

6. In thirty seconds, how many words can you find to describe a boy who has lost his pet?

7. Make up a four-line poem to tell your friend how glad you are she came over to see you.

8. You confided your friend's secret to someone else after she specifically told you never to share it. She finds out. How would she act toward you the next time she sees you? What could you do to change her feelings?

9. You felt very bad that you left a friend out of a game you were playing with two other girls. How can you tell her you're sorry? With pictures? with music? with rhymes?

10. Your friend comes to school looking sad and mad, and he won't talk to you. (You don't think he's mad at you because just yesterday afternoon everything between you was great.) What do you think is wrong with him? How would you ask him about it? What can you do to help?

SEXUALITY:
"Look at this big rip in my underpants—WHOOEE!!"

Alexa and Charlotte, both six (Performer/Adapter and Strong-Willed Child/Naysayer) were always leaving their first-grade class together to go to the bathroom. One day the teacher, annoyed with their prolonged absence, went in to see what was taking so long. The two girls had their pants off and were "bumping butts," as they called it. The teacher's outraged reaction caused Charlotte to explain that they were just comparing the rips in their underpants. Giggle.

What's Really Going On?

Since Alexa's mother just had a baby, the family has been talking about the differences between dads and moms, boys and girls. Showing and comparing body parts, talking about bathroom activities, and sharing a bathroom create a lot of excitement for some children at this age who are usually aware of underlying feelings of sexuality anyway.

The girls are also interested in comparing their own bodies to those of their mothers. Where will the breasts, the body hair, the curves come from, and how?

By touching and comparing the sights and smells of their bodies, children are trying to gain mastery over something they don't understand: the mysteries of sex. Within a year or so they will probably put this curiosity aside as they focus more on their personal competencies and their interests and abilities. They will lose their fascination, at least until preadolescence, when this issue will emerge again.

Not every child will be so blatant about her sexual interests. A loner who doesn't participate readily in group activities and who is shy with friends may masturbate. A pair of creative, sensitive girls may spend a lot of time playing dress-up, and although they may take off their street clothes during the course of their game, they may not spend much time on overtly sexual behavior.

Your Child/Your Role

HAS YOUR CHILD EVER:

- Pulled down his pants or his underwear in public?
- Interrupted your shower with some flimsy excuse in order to see or try to touch your genitals?
- Spent the afternoon with a friend drawing numerous renditions of bodily functions and sexual activity?

The best thing you can do in such instances is not to act shocked or to punish the child. This doesn't mean you have to condone the behavior, and if your child is spending unusual amounts of time preoccupied with sexuality, you should actively try to discourage it by pointing him toward another physical activity that will rechannel his energy. Remember not to color your suggestion with any hint of shame or blame—just offer him alternatives and he'll probably be enthusiastic about one or several of them.

You'll know if your child is concentrating too much on bodily functions if he or she frequently wants to undress or touch your own or a friend's body in inappropriate ways. You might also notice an intense interest in sexual elements in real life or on television. If your child can't stop talking about the topic, it's possible that there might be too much sexual stimulation in the home. Review your policies about privacy for toileting or bathing, and for undressing. Everyone's privacy is important, and you may have to emphasize this now.

Think about other activities that are "out in the open" right now. Do you and your spouse touch or kiss in ways that might be unsettling or confusing to your child? A six- or seven-year-old is not mature enough to consider the possibilities inherent in adult or even sibling nudity without a lot of anxiety. And because basically he's aware that it's not socially acceptable, he may lock the door on you if he's busy acting out sexually, either alone or with a friend.

If your child continues to be overly preoccupied with sexual matters, you might wish to consult a psychologist to brainstorm about other events going on in the home or in your child's life that might have caused him to focus so heavily on sexual matters.

WANNA BE MY FRIEND?"

How You Can Encourage
Appropriate Social Skills

The social skills you want to develop in order to work out this issue have to do with following rules and maintaining group activities. You might consider planning an activity for playdates that will take the children outside or involve them in doing something with you. They may want to use "bathroom language" while they're with you, and if you can stand it, it's probably easier to have a time period during which it's allowed rather than to squelch it completely.

If your child is spending a lot of time in this kind of pursuit with a child of the same sex, it isn't necessarily a cause for alarm. Most girls of all social styles, for instance, will do their experimentation with another girl, because they tend to play exclusively with girls at this point.

DEVELOPING A SENSE OF RIGHT AND WRONG:
"I don't have to listen to you—you're bad!"

Jenny and Eileen, both six and a half, were best friends. Jenny, the product of two understanding but not permissive parents, was a Strong-Willed Thinker. Eileen, a Fragile Flower/Follower, had a tough-guy mother who expected her children to do what she asked them to or be disciplined if they did not. Both girls were at a stage where their own "internal policeman"—underdeveloped but certainly present—was causing conflict between their impulses and their obligations.

Jenny was at Eileen's house for a playdate when Eileen's mother asked the girls to return a cake plate to a neighbor and come right back. After performing their errand, however, Jenny decided she wanted to stop by her house and say hello to her mother. However, this would have involved their crossing a street and they hadn't been given permission. The girls got into an argument about following the rules.

Eileen was terrified that she'd be punished for disobeying. Jenny was disgusted with Eileen's compliance: "I don't have to do what your mommy says. You're dumb to be so scared," she declared.

"I don't have to listen to you—you're *bad!*" Eileen retorted as she started back to her own house.

The girls refused to speak to each other when Eileen's mother tried to intervene, and each blamed the other for the incident.

What's Really Going On?

These children are torn between their delight in independence—being entrusted with an errand alone in the neighborhood—and their anxiety about being given too much freedom. Each strongly reflects her parents' different style of behavior: Jenny sees the opportunity for breaking out; Eileen is paralyzed at the thought of crossing a forbidden street. They each have a set of internalized rules that aren't flexible enough to allow them to compromise just yet.

These two girls have very different social styles—one likes to watch and wait and follow rules; the other is a more daring explorer. But imagine two children with similar styles dealing with the same issue.

Suppose Diane, a demanding child, taunts her friend Crystal not just into crossing the street but into going on a tour of the neighborhood! Maybe Crystal combines a healthy cautiousness with her sense of enthuasism about joining an activity. Crystal agrees to break the rules and walks a forbidden block with her friend. But in the process of misbehaving, she analyzes the situation and sizes up the consequences. As a child with some leadership ability of her own, she backs down with the excuse that she's bored with the excursion and has decided to go home, and she urges Diane to do the same.

Whether one child leads and one follows or whether

both act as leaders, it's clear that their emerging sense of right and wrong—as well as the family backgrounds they bring to the experience—are in conflict.

Your Child/Your Role

HAS YOUR CHILD EVER:

- Deliberately broken a long-standing rule, knowing he will be punished?
- Created a special set of restrictions and regulations for a friend or a younger sibling?
- Told a baby-sitter or a grandparent that she's allowed to do certain things she knows are forbidden?

If you have set age-appropriate limits for your child earlier in her life, you can expect to see her setting them for herself now. Not that she will stick consistently to her own rules *or* yours!

This is a time of experimentation, and one day's "perfect" conduct may be countered the next with a slew of infractions. Don't be surprised if you hear from a grandparent, baby-sitter, teacher, or older sibling that your model of decorum is "running amuck." The reverse may happen too: your "wild child" at home may be perfectly behaved with the sitter or grandparent.

Another social skill that's blossoming right now is leadership ability, and you can certainly encourage this. Show a child you trust her to make her own decisions (within certain set parameters), and she will start making good ones most of the time. You might allow her to decide which two programs she'll watch on Saturday morning if she agrees to turn the set off afterward; you might let her prepare her own snack when she comes home from school if she agrees to keep the junk food to a minimum.

Remember that it takes everyone a while to get their internal policeman to function properly. You can help—particularly when someone else is in charge—by conferring about styles of discipline and punishment. If after your child comes home from a friend's house, she reports that another parent has allowed her to do something that you would not allow, talk to the other parent so that you can work it out together.

How You Can Encourage Appropriate Social Skills

You should certainly discuss rules and concepts of right and wrong with your children as they start spending time with their friends' parents. It's also a good idea to know a little about the other parents' standards and rules. You can tactfully ask, for example, how much TV they allow their child to watch, or whether they permit their child to walk alone to the mini-park around the corner. Maybe each of you can agree to alter your styles a little if the occasion should necessitate it.

Try not to stick to a belief that "the way we do things always goes." If you ruthlessly enforce your own style, you may reinforce your child's need to obey slavishly, and as she grows, it may be harder for her to make up her mind for herself.

Conversely if your child has a well-developed sense of self-esteem, she might start rebelling against your dominant personality in an attempt to let her own social style shine. A child who always pushes against the limits you've set can become very negative and disagreeable. She might dig in her heels and refuse to cooperate even in situations where you and she probably would have agreed.

Or she might turn inward, becoming obsessive about some made-up rituals of her own, such as always stacking her library books in a circle on the floor or always having to go to the bathroom twice before she leaves the house. This would be her way of ordering her universe the way she wanted it.

If you see things going in a negative direction too often, it may be time for you to soften your rules a bit. Don't assume that every decision has to end at loggerheads—instead choose your battles wisely, over issues you consider important for your child and your family. Review Chapter Three, on parenting, and do some real soul-searching. If you have felt a need to exert a lot of discipline and have become authoritarian without realizing it, you can correct your tendency to overdo. Each time you come to a point of contention with your child, listen carefully to his point of view and try to articulate his feelings aloud in your own words.

You might say, "You really act like I'm going to chop your head off when I tell you a playdate's over and I want you to get ready to go home." This kind of exaggeration may be just what your child needs so that he can start to express himself. Maybe he thinks you've been been too abrupt or that you don't approve of his having fun. When you know how he feels, you can explain your rules in a way that your child can understand and accept—or at least is willing to try on for size. This kind of dialogue may make it easier the next time you pick him up at a friend's house and he's aware that he only gets one warning to put his shoes and coat on.

But suppose you tend to be a permissive parent. If you are inconsistent about setting limits for your child and give her too much free rein, it will be increasingly difficult for her to exert her own self-control in a situation where she must make decisions by herself. She may have trouble learning to understand and trust friends whose ideas are not in line with hers. If she tends to take things personally and isn't especially good at teamwork, she could conceivably find herself shunned by boys and girls, who might see her as a loner.

A kid who always gets his own way and is never expected

to give something up might become very selfish. He might find it impossible to progress smoothly into the next, more bonded, stage of friendship, where empathy is at a premium.

Children at this stage need to respect one another's internal policemen as well as their own, and this of course takes a certain amount of empathy. When your child gets practice in giving something up for the friendship, such as forgoing a trip inside the fun house at an amusement park because it scares her friend, or agreeing to ride her friend's bike with training wheels instead of her own new speedy two-wheeler, she will eventually get the idea that her momentary impulses should not be paramount in every situation.

And she'll reap the rewards later, in the closeness of her friendships and the respect of her parents.

WARNING SIGNS THAT YOUR CHILD MIGHT NEED HELP

You should be alert to any problems that your child is experiencing with the issues we've discussed in this chapter. Of course it's perfectly normal for all children to go through rocky periods, but they shouldn't be having trouble all the time. If they are, consult Chapter Nine, "Children Who Can't Reach Out."

In addition, ask yourself the following questions about your child. If the answer to several of the items is affirmative *on a regular basis*, your child may need professional help:

- Is it hard for your child to make friends in any situation? Does she get hostile, alienate other children, or ignore them completely?
- Does every playdate end in a fight? Does she often seem to create situations deliberately that will lead to conflict?
- When given the choice, does your child always refuse a playdate and prefer to play by himself?

- Can he *never* see a friend's point of view?
- Is she overly interested in sex play?
- Is he always submissive in friendships?
- Is he always dominant in his friendships?

With the information you now have about your child's friendships from five to seven years of age, you can assist and encourage the best friendship skills for this age and pave the way for the more sophisticated relationships that are to come.

7

FRIENDSHIP AMONG CHILDREN AGES EIGHT TO TEN

"Can I invite Tom for a sleepover, Mom?" asked eight-year-old Leo. "He's my best friend at camp. Since he just broke his arm, I'll sleep on the sofa bed and he can have my bed." You do a double-take and immediately agree. The idea of Leo giving up his own comfort for a hurt friend is a first, and you wisely decide not to question his altruistic offer.

"How could you tell Rosalie's mom the secret I told you last week? You are the dumbest mother in the whole world!" You stare at your ten-year-old in horror. What happened to the compliant, easygoing child who never talks back to you?

"I wish Debby was coming to my party, but I bet she said no because I didn't invite her sister, Patty. But Patty's such a baby, and I wanted to invite just my friends." You nod, impressed with your nine-year-old's take on the situation, sad for her because she'll be missing her friend, but realizing it was her decision and she's got to live with it.

HOW YOUR CHILD GROWS SOCIALLY
FROM AGES EIGHT TO TEN

This is a volatile period for friendships. Children of this age are straddling two eras—the five-to-seven-year-old period of making friends by sharing actual, concrete things, and the preadolescent period, where friends are selected because of abstract qualities such as trust, support, tact, patience, and concern. You'll find that your eight-to-ten-year-old is sometimes cranky and upset about friendship issues that you thought she'd resolved a year ago. Yet at other times you'll be amazed at the sophistication of her social abilities, often seeming so much wiser than her years that you fear she's growing up too fast.

Friendships at this stage begin to resemble the kinds of relationships we have as adults. Whereas younger children enjoy inviting friends over regardless of whether or not the feelings are reciprocated, the eight-to-ten-year-old has just become conscious of mutuality. If the other guy isn't perceived as returning the strong feelings your child is putting out, the friendship may founder. There is an unspoken agreement that interdependence in a relationship is crucial.

There is also a big difference now in the way your child's social style affects her friendships. No matter how well you thought you had your son or daughter pegged as a "Thinker with Fragile Flower qualities" or a "Team Player who tends to be a Boss under stress," you will see now that those characteristics become less important. This is not to say that your introvert will turn into an extrovert (although she may!), but that the temperamental qualities that fixed your child's adaptation to others blend more smoothly and become more fluid.

WHAT MAKES PARENTS ANXIOUS?

You were used to making decisions for your child. You were the one to arrange all the playdates, and you were in charge of structuring her daily and weekly schedule. But now things are changing, and the eight-to-ten-year-old's newfound independence is difficult for some parents to handle.

You may find that the good-natured Adapter, who could play with anyone, has become more selective. Your suggestion that she go knock on Megan's door if she's bored may be met with total disdain, although she used to play contentedly with the next-door neighbor's child all the time. "But Mom," your daughter will protest, "you know she uses the most terrible language and always picks a fight over the dumbest little things. How could you want me to play with her?"

You may see the truth in her words when she says them privately to you, but still be concerned that she may snub someone she used to treat kindly. You may be surprised to see, however, that your child is now able to keep her negative opinions to herself because her empathy skills are stronger. If you don't interfere, she may actually say no to an invitation with tact and grace.

In contrast, your intervention in her life may be bitterly criticized as she tries to separate her social skills from your imposed rules. Your extroverted Team Player may retreat to the backyard to shoot baskets alone and may refuse to come in to dinner when called; your Performer dancer may swear she'll never dance again because she's just realized that some other girl in her class deserves the lead in the show more than she does.

These confusions are to be expected at a time when boys and girls are not clingy babies anymore, but aren't yet independent adolescents either. You will have to watch and wait, expect the unexpected, and enjoy the changes, the mishaps, the growth that comes. And it will come!

WHAT ISSUES ARE PARAMOUNT
FOR YOUR CHILD RIGHT NOW?

The main friendship issues for this age group are:

- The beginning of altruism and being less egocentric
- The selection of a best friend
- Giving emotional support, patience, tact, and concern instead of giving objects
- A sense that trust should not be violated in a friendship
- A shift in the dependent relationship to parents

Children in the eight-to-ten age group are now able to be *less egocentric and more altruistic*—at least some of the time. Whereas before, they generally counted someone a friend if *they* profited from it emotionally and physically, now they are willing to put their own demands aside for the sake of being with someone they truly like and who likes them. They are now aware that the world is filled with other individuals with different egos and different standards who add spice and color to their life. This ability to be less self-involved allows them to relinquish the need to get their way all the time.

They are now ready to *select a best friend*. Harry Stack Sullivan, the noted American psychiatrist, wrote that the preference for spending time with a "chum," as he termed it, indicated a new spurt in a child's emotional maturity. This is time of life when a special bond with one other person is desired and cultivated. There is a mutuality of interests and closeness between these two. This is not to say that your child will abandon all other friendships. But you will find that this relationship is more complex than his friendships with his other pals because it is based on a beginning of appreciation of the unique psychological characteristics of the other.

The best friend your child gravitates toward could easily be a companion he's known for the past five years or so. But the *quality* of the relationship will take on a deeper dimension, because now these children are ready to appreciate one another's personalities, differences, and quirks. They are ready to trust one another with secrets, and, what may be more important, they are ready to work through disappointments that may occur within the relationship. They can suffer a break, patch it up, and move on. You may find that your child is mature enough to talk out minor problems with the close friend who has wronged him.

Whereas you used to see your child playing with another in relation to objects they could trade back and forth, now you will see *more abstract giving* as kids of this age are able to express their empathy in the form of concern, tact, patience, and support. They are also better able to anticipate another child's reaction to their behavior.

The flip side of this heightened sensitivity is that *serious violations of trust* will be judged much more harshly. A friend who "rats on" your child may no longer be considered worthy of consideration for another playdate. You may be surprised when your introverted Shy Child or extroverted Adapter suddenly starts holding grudges.

The final issue that concerns children of this age group is *separation from parents*. The pull away from family that begins at this age and continues through adolescence can be a shocker, especially if you had felt you have a close, intimate bond with your child. You still do—but the difference is that your child is now trying to establish herself in the world as an entity without you. She has come to a point in her own maturity where she is able to make use of the internal policeman she began to develop in the five-to-seven-year-old stage. Now she has enough experience internalizing your rules and regulations, and she is ready to fine-tune them so that they can become her own.

Now that your child is older, your Social Skills Kit needs to be updated. By the time your child is eight, you will find that verbal and interactive games are more effective than the play materials suggested in Chapter Four. (If your child has highly developed social intelligence, she may be ready to talk about friendship issues at the age of six or seven, in which case you can switch to this verbal kit earlier.)

The Social Skills Verbal Kit for the older child consists of two sections.

Section 1. Find the Hidden Emotion:
What Does Your Friend Really Mean
When He Says . . . ?

It's sometimes difficult for your child to pick up the real meanings behind his friends' statements. The purpose of this exercise is to encourage him to look deeper than the surface words he hears. If your child can understand the subtext, he'll find it easier to connect with his friends. He may also improve at figuring out verbal and nonverbal communications that used to confuse him.

You can explain to your child that understanding what someone else is *really* saying underneath the obvious words is a vital step in being a good friend. He will still have to find out for sure what problem his friend is going through before he can offer help. You can also point out that sometimes an alligator is just an alligator! In other words, sometimes there's nothing being hidden at all, and what you see is what you get.

Have your child read one of the following examples aloud, then discuss with her what might be the underlying feeling.

1. "Boy, the whole neighborhood must have heard my mom and dad fighting last night—it was like a kung fu movie!"

Ask her what she thinks the speaker was saying. In the first example she might read in an excited voice, because the words imply noise and action. Then ask her to read it with the tone of voice that several different friends might give it. As she experiments with the words as they might sound coming from different people, she may stumble on the hidden relevance herself. If she doesn't, you can ask pointed questions: "Would you be embarrassed if Mommy and I were fighting so loudly that everyone could hear? Do you think that the speaker in this example is frightened about what's going on with his parents? Suppose his parents fight all the time and he's worried about them getting a divorce? What could you say to make him feel better?"

Try the next examples with your child, first trying to elicit the superficial meaning, then the hidden meaning, and finally what your child could do to help her friend who'd said this to her.

2. "I swam so far out, the lifeguards had to come get me! It was neat!" (Is he anxious that he might have drowned? How can you tell him that he took a stupid risk and you care enough about him to hope that he doesn't do it again?)
3. "I really like it at your house. I think I'll move in." (Is she upset about something at home? What might be going on between her and her parents? How do you feel about her being close to your parents?)
4. "Christine said you think fat people are gross. Do you think I'm fat?" (Does your friend feel betrayed? Does she want to know where she stands with you? Do you want to tell her honestly? Can you use tact to patch up the relationship?)
5. "You're a better artist (writer, team player, bike rider) than I am." (Does your friend feel insecure and is she looking for praise? How could you help her feel better about herself?)
6. "I don't want to ask stupid Mr. Jones if we can play ball at recess. Why don't you ask him?" (Is your friend afraid of Mr. Jones? Does he always shift responsibility to someone else? How do you feel about shouldering that burden?)

7. "My little brother threw up so much last night, it covered the whole rug! (laughing) We all got to ride to the hospital behind this screaming ambulance. Wow, I didn't know cars could go that fast." (Is your friend anxious about his brother's illness? How could you help him find out about his brother's condition?)

8. "I can't play with you today. My mom says too many play-dates with the same friend aren't a good idea." (Is your friend telling you that he doesn't really want to play with you? Or is it his mother's fault? How could you get your friend to be honest with you? And to find out if something went wrong in the relationship that would make him not want to play with you?)

9. "I was the only girl in the whole class not to be invited to that stupid party. I'm really glad because I have much better things to do that day!" (Does your friend feel neglected and sad? What could you say to make her feel better?)

Section 2.   Peer-Pressure Puzzles

You will probably find enough examples within your child's life to discuss sticky ethical decisions that may trouble him—particularly when "everyone else" is acting a certain way or doing a certain activity and he doesn't want to be left out. But the following puzzles for the older child are good practice for a variety of possible situations he may encounter in the next few years. You may want to wait to use some of the items, those that refer to R-rated movies or dating, until your child is in the ten-to-twelve-year-old group. If he's having trouble figuring out what he might do and why, you might want to bring up incidents from your own childhood where you had to deal with peer pressure. When he knows that his parents aren't infallible and felt just as much ambivalence over "doing the right thing" as he does, he may find it easier to make his own choices.

Let him rehearse his ethical choices with you, and try not to impose your standards on his decisions. If he chooses to go along with the crowd because it's "really cool," you can ask him to continue the scenario and figure out what might happen to him and his friends if he makes a choice to try to get away with something. You can brainstorm with him to come up with his own creative options, so that instead of going along with his peers or saying no and walking away from the situation, he may be able to offer a new, equally "cool," activity for them to do together.

What Should You Do If . . . ?

1. A group of popular girls pushes you to break a date with a shy friend so that you can go ice-skating with them.
2. A bunch of kids want to booby-trap a "nerd's" desk with a cherry bomb, which will go off when he opens it. They ask you to help out.
3. You are hanging out after school with three boys from the cool crowd. One boy takes out a pack of cigarettes and they all light up. Then they offer one to you.
4. All the girls are wearing holes in the knees of their jeans. One of them hands you a scissors in the bathroom and snipes that you're such a mama's girl, you wouldn't dare do it.
5. A boy in your class puts his arm around you and asks you to go to the movies with him alone. You feel uncomfortable with him, but you know that other girls are dating.
6. You are in a local deli with two friends you like a lot, and they start playing a game to see who can sneak the most stuff off the shelves and into their pockets. One of them sticks some gum into your pocket and urges you to continue filling it.
7. A few of your friends start writing on the bathroom stall doors at the library. One hands you an extra pen and asks why you're not doing it.
8. Four of your friends get a math test in advance from a kid

in last year's class. They tell you you can copy the answers, too, and tease you for hesitating.

9. Three older boys you know decide to go to an R-rated movie and lie to their parents about being at one of the guys' houses during that time. They want you to join them.

A SENSE OF ALTRUISM:
"I'll swim in the shallow end as long as I can be with you."

Randy, at eight, was a Performer and, when under stress or feeling insecure, could be something of a Boss. She was one of the best young swimmers in her family's swim club, which had produced some great national competitors. But her new friend, Marissa, a Thinker and Adapter, didn't swim at all. Randy promised to spend the afternoon in the shallow end with her—she said they could just talk and hang out in the water.

After about an hour Randy asked Marissa if she'd be upset if she went over to the deep end to do a few dives with her swim-team friends.

Marissa scowled and sighed. "I should have known you wouldn't want to stay in the shallow end with me."

"I'll be right back." Randy ran over and got a kickboard and an inner tube from the lifeguard and brought them to Marissa. Then she dodged away before her friend could complain.

Randy's mom, watching from the sidelines, could see how much her daughter wanted to stay with her more accomplished peers. She was tempted to go and tell her daughter that her time in the deep end was up, but decided to let Randy handle it.

Randy had been gone about ten minutes when she looked over and saw Marissa sitting on the side of the shallow end, looking bored. Then she heard her pals telling her it was her turn to dive. She told them to wait a second, then went back to Marissa.

"Do you mind if I stay in the deep end a little longer?" she asked.

Marissa shrugged and didn't look at her. "Oh, do whatever you want. It doesn't matter to me."

Randy was totally torn. She looked back at her other friends, who were having a terrific time on the diving board and splashing in the water. Then she looked at Marissa. "Hey," she said to her friend. "I'm going to teach you to swim, okay?"

Marissa looked puzzled, then smiled. "Okay," she agreed.

What's Really Going On?

This eight-year-old has begun to shift her friendship priorities. The exchange of concrete items, although it still goes on, is not the measure of how much children at this age like one another, nor is it usually a way to make up after they've had a fight. The older child realizes that giving up something of her own in order to spend pleasant time with a person she values is more important than always getting her own way or having things "be fair."

When she was younger, Randy might have found it impossible to spend an afternoon at the pool not being the "star." And even now, staying out of the diving area and not getting accolades for doing what she does so well isn't easy for her. She's clearly torn between her desire to stand out among her accomplished friends and her promise to come right back to Marissa. She is being generous even though she doesn't *feel* generous.

She doesn't demand that her friend conform to her wishes—the Boss part of Randy's personality has blended into a more well-rounded social style. She actually anticipates Marissa's annoyed reaction to her taking time for herself, so she is extra careful about Marissa's feelings and well-being while she's away. Randy gets Marissa a kickboard and an inner tube to play with as if to say, "These concrete things will take my place while I'm away." And finally Randy solves her own problem by coming up with an activity that will be exciting for both her and Marissa. If she teaches her buddy to swim, they can eventually both go to the deep end.

Notice that Randy has a lot of important social skills that assist her in giving up her own immediate pleasure for the afternoon with Marissa. She has a strong sense of enthusiasm and fun and an ability to follow rules (especially her own!). She also has empathy for her friend, an ability to analyze situations and find solutions, and, perhaps most important of all, she has a good sense of timing. She knows *when* to be with her friend, *when* and how to separate, and *when* to come back. She might only have had the potential for these a year ago; yet now they are quite fully developed.

It's also interesting to look at Marissa's skills. She is the follower rather than the leader in this particular instance, but she holds all the cards. By just sitting in the shallow end, acknowledging that she can't swim and that Randy must come to her if she wants to be with her, she shows that she is capable of exerting her will to get what she needs and is confident about her strong position in the relationship. Since Randy chooses to spend time with her, even though she lacks the physical abilities that Randy usually admires in friends, she must have a lot of deeper qualities to recommend her.

If the girls were both Fragile Flowers, they might have been tripping over themselves to apologize for what they couldn't give each other. Yet each one seems secure in her participation in this friendship. Randy's mother didn't have to worry about her daughter letting her friend down.

Your Child/Your Role

HAS YOUR CHILD EVER:

- Been accommodating to a friend, then become furious if that friend didn't appreciate it or give back the same treatment?
- Invited a friend over because he thought he *should*, then acted rude or totally ignored him?
- Offered to call a sick friend, then forgotten to do so?
- Switched within a few brief minutes from being a truly giving individual to being selfish and whiny?

The most crucial social skill you'd like your child to develop around the issue of altruism is empathy and the willingness and ability to participate. Once he's developed these, the other skills on the list will come more easily. It's as if you were suggesting that he "say yes" to life—not blindly of course, but with a goal in mind. Delayed gratification, or rewards that don't seem awfully exciting on the surface, are difficult for anyone, of any age, to accept. This is particularly true for a child who is a bit of a Naysayer or who is really Strong-Willed.

The willingness to give something up with no concrete reward in sight takes a lot of practice. Don't expect your child to get it immediately. For example, you might have a team situation where the coach asks your child, a regular player on the softball team, to give up a turn at bat or to play the outfield so that a new kid can practice. If your child is a Naysayer or even a Team Player, he might grudgingly give the other child what he was asked but might take it out on you later by talking back or refusing to do his regular household chores. It's always safer for a child to express his bad moods to his family than to another child or an outside authority figure, such as a teacher or a coach. You may find that you become the unwitting target in many circumstances because your child just doesn't know how to deal with his anger toward others. This is a good time to go back to Chapter Six and work on "Developing Your Child's Empathy," since having empathy forms a solid basis for altruism.

This is a crucial time in parent-child relations. Since your eight-to-ten-year-old is now on his own a great deal, out in the world without your guidance or presence, try to find out what your child's feelings are and what might have triggered them *before* you reprimand or punish him for an infraction of long-standing rules.

Randy's mother, for example, trusts her daughter's developmental process and leaves her alone to make her own choice about staying in the deep end or going back to Marissa. If she were on either end of the parenting spectrum—a Worrier or a Tough Guy—she could subvert Randy's good intentions. A mother who refused to take the girls to the pool because she *knew* her daughter wouldn't stay in the shallow water, for example, or a mother who criticized Randy for briefly leaving the scene to do a few dives would have made a Strong-Willed Child fight back, defending her position. In order for the eight-to-ten-year-old to see that the benefits of altruism toward others outweigh the sacrifices, parents must allow their children freedom and time to experiment on their own.

In addition, be sure to reinforce the idea that your child's feelings have value and that no one should be able to use him or take advantage of him. Children who have been taught that they *ought* to do something or feel a certain way may have a difficult time with balancing their own needs and the needs of others. Naturally we all have certain obligations in life, but you don't want to load your child with the burden of giving and never taking, regardless of the feelings involved. That way lies the danger of being manipulated and controlled by other, stronger-willed children.

If your child tends to do what others have asked of her, because of either anxiety or low self-esteem, you can and should teach her to protect herself. This is particularly urgent with girls today who may find themselves in adolescence in potential date- and acquaintance-rape situations. Girls—or boys—who have grown up always doing what they're told can be coerced into saying yes regardless of their true feelings. These children need some work on skills that emphasize negotiation and problem solving. You can do some role-playing with your child and urge her to stand up for her rights. (See "Social Skills Verbal Kit, Section 2. Peer Pressure Puzzles," page 154.)

Let's assume your daughter is Marissa and she doesn't have the assertiveness we saw in her at the swimming pool. Marissa is now a Shy Child who can be a bit of a Fragile Flower when under stress. Suppose Randy is always taking advantage of her. You could say, "I notice sometimes that Randy is awfully bossy. I'll be Randy, telling you what we're going to do at the swimming pool this afternoon, and you'll answer me back." By encouraging playfulness in this situation and letting her think on her feet, you'll show her that there are a variety of responses to every situation. And she doesn't always have to let her friend take the lead.

FINDING A BEST FRIEND:
"You're the only human being on the planet I'd ever tell this to."

John and Al had met in day care, and they had played together until Al's family relocated so that Al's father could start a new job. But when the boys were nine, Al's parents divorced, and Al and his mother moved back to the old neighborhood. The boys seemed to re-form a tight bond, even though Al had repeated first grade in his other school, so the boys were a year apart academically. Al, an Adapter and Team Player, was a lot more outgoing than John, who was an academic Thinker and could be a Fragile Flower in difficult circumstances.

Though both boys had groups of friends in their own classes, they preferred each other's company so much that they planned their vacation together. John's parents took Al with them to their summer cabin, and the boys spent two weeks happily making wooden boats out of Popsicle sticks and pieces of an old crate. The boys fought occasionally, but they always knew how to make up promptly. They never complained of boredom or asked what they should do next. They weren't at all uncomfortable being silly together—John felt free to be himself with Al, even though he tended to be hyperaware of what other boys thought about him.

John's mother heard a lot of commotion in the bathroom one night and opened the door to find the boys in their bathing suits in the tub. They were sailing their boats, populated now by a variety of G.I. Joe dolls and a turtle they had caught in the pond outside their house. She couldn't figure out if this was a war game or a pretend visit to another planet. The boys were jabbering in some made-up language and laughing hysterically.

John's mother couldn't put her finger on what seemed so unusual about this scene, but it occurred to her later that John would never play this way with any other child—he was always so careful about not appearing silly or babyish.

What's Really Going On?

John trusts Al. Al trusts John. It makes no difference that they're in different grades or have different sets of friends or different social styles. There is something inherently *right* about their connection to one another, which, at this point in their lives they couldn't duplicate with anyone else.

These two nine-year-olds have each discovered a "soul mate," someone with whom they can act silly, share information, and even complain about parents. They also have no trouble amusing themselves for long periods of time without guidance or supervision. They can behave more like family than like guests in one another's homes—making decisions, arguing and resolving squabbles, changing roles seamlessly so that one or the other alternately leads or follows.

A year ago or so the boys couldn't have made a distinction between the personalities and strengths of each friend. John might easily have made the error of asking Joe, a Team Player without a great deal of imagination, if he'd play war with him in the bathtub or make up a new language. He would have been rebuffed and not understood why. The Fragile Flower part of him would have come to the fore, and he might have felt really hurt. Now, however, his social-style blend has come together, and he is also sophisticated enough to be able to see the unique characteristics of each friend. Lots of adults have trouble with that!

Your Child/Your Role

HAS YOUR CHILD EVER:

- Neglected schoolwork, after-school activities, or family events to be with one friend?
- Started to dress or talk like his best friend?
- Stated that everyone else is wrong (about any and every subject!), and only his best friend knows the answers?

Having a best friend can be a wonderful experience for a child, but as with any new passion, he or she may overdo it or do it awkwardly. At an age when children are struggling with separating from their families and wishing to be independent, it's common for them to switch allegiances and try to model themselves after their friend. Parents constantly hear, "I don't have to take out the garbage because Vince doesn't." Or, "Judith wears short skirts to school—why can't I?"

Sometimes it happens that your child may misperceive the real nature of the relationship. There are instances where the deep feelings are one-sided. Suppose your child is all excited about having a new "best friend," but over the course of watching them together and listening to reports of what they do together, you discern that the feeling is not mutual. If a Fragile Flower or a Follower really thinks he's found his soul mate, but the Performer or Strong-Willed Child he's hooked up with considers your child to be just another pal, severely hurt feelings can result.

You can help out here by getting your child to talk about what he expects from this relationship that he's not getting. Then you can have him list all the things he *does* get from this friendship. Maybe he's troubled by the fact that his social style clashes with that of his friend. The child he thinks he likes may not be on his wavelength, or he may be misinterpreting signals the other child is giving. He may complain that though he loves sitting and reading quietly on the windowseat next to his friend, every time he tries it, his buddy keeps interrupting, telling jokes and ruining the mood. Try working with him on the "Find the Hidden Emotion" questions in your Social Skills Verbal Kit, Section 1, to see if you can make it easier for him to understand the messages that others are giving him. Maybe the other child is a poor reader and is embarrassed to be asked to do this activity; maybe he comes from a family where everyone talks all the time, so sitting quietly makes him uncomfortable.

If your child has narrowed his sights to one friend but the relationship isn't working out, you may want to encourage your child to get together with several children whose social skills and style may be more in sync with his. You could plan a cooking and dinner party with one friend, a museum trip with another, a roller-blading date with a third. You could also allow your child to plan her own lunch (or snack) party for several people she really likes. This way you can help your child experience a variety of friendships and consider which are best for her.

If your child hasn't found a best friend, you might want to consider whether you yourself may be unintentionally discouraging him from doing so. If you happen to be a very social family, with a wide mix of acquaintances, you may subtly give the message that it's not all right to keep all your eggs in a single basket. Naturally if John kept bringing Al home for playdates and his mother kept asking why he was excluding other children from his life, John would get the message that it wasn't all right to cultivate this one friend.

You may frown on your child's chum because of some deep-seated memories of your own. Go back to Chapter Three and see whether you may have some long-standing feelings of jealousy, remembering times when a tight couple of pals excluded you from their secrets and special times. It can be hard to view your child in a close relationship with a best friend when you never had one yourself.

Or maybe your child appears to be *too* attached to his soul mate and you fear he may be losing his grasp on his own identity. It's perfectly natural for a kid of this age to want to be "just like" his best friend, but if he mindlessly keeps mimicking a pal's behavior, speech, and dress, you can call him on it. The familiar old question "If Johnny jumped off the Empire State Building, would you?" sometimes brings perspective back. This prodding should cause a chuckle, and you may see your child back off from his intense involvement.

If your child persists in imitating another child, this may be a sign that he is confused or troubled about making his own decisions. Giving your child a little more responsibility around the house may bolster his sense of himself. Encouraging playdates with children he's not so attached to will allow him to experiment more regarding when to lead and follow in a relationship.

There are children who do not find a best friend. Some kids, especially those whose social style tends to be extroverted, feel more comfortable joining teams and clubs and keeping relationships more diversified. This is fine, too, because knowing how to get along with many different types can be invaluable in later life. The child who excels as a leader and who is great at maintaining group activities may forgo the best friend for a circle of several rather close pals.

If at this age your child is not connecting with any other children, you may wish to seek professional evaluation to discuss any family problems or perhaps a subtle learning disability that makes it hard for your child to pick up nonverbal cues or to react to others with empathy. (See Chapter Nine, "Children Who Can't Reach Out.")

GIVING EMOTIONAL SUPPORT
RATHER THAN EXCHANGING OBJECTS:
"I didn't know you felt that way too.
Maybe I can help."

Ralph, almost ten, had always been an active, physical Team Player, but this year he was going through rough times and had become a Fragile Flower. Up until now his closest friend had been his brother—two years older than he—and his other pals had been mainly acquaintances he knew from playing sports on teams.

Ralph couldn't tell anyone, because he thought they'd think he was wimpy, but he was becoming really nervous about switching from elementary to middle school the following year. He was in the playground one Saturday, shooting baskets by himself, when another kid, Frank, came and asked if he could play one-on-one with him.

Ralph had known Frank since first grade and had always thought of him as a weird kid, an unpredictable Naysayer who wore his shoelaces untied as some kind of fashion statement.

"Not bad," Frank nodded as Ralph rimmed one and it just made it into the basket. "Give it a little more push at the end." He showed Ralph how to palm the ball and then send it flying. "When we move over to middle school, all the geeks in the older classes are gonna shove us right off the courts unless we're *really* good. We gotta be good."

Ralph suddenly realized that Frank was as worried as he was about moving up to the "big kids' school." "We could practice together," Ralph offered. "C'mon, take a couple dribbles, pass it to me, and I'll dunk it. You move faster than me, but I'm taller."

Frank grinned, then did as Ralph suggested. It worked.

What's Really Going On?

These two boys have banded together to give each other moral support as they face a difficult time in their lives. Although they probably wouldn't have become friends two years ago—Ralph always kept his distance from Frank because he thought he acted and dressed in an unconventional way—now they have a goal to meet together.

The boys help each other in a variety of ways. Frank shares his feelings with Ralph about "the way it's gonna be" and the fact that he feels unprepared to handle the changes to come. And he also tactfully corrects Ralph's basketball technique with constructive criticism that will help them both to get ahead socially in their new environment. Ralph encourages his friend by suggesting they practice with one another. The unspoken message between them is "This is really scary. It'll be better if we face it together."

Girls are more likely than boys to express those feelings of vulnerability, as well as their need for someone to care and be concerned about them. An introvert, a Follower or Thinker may have a highly developed awareness of what she has now and what she may be losing by growing up. A friend with similar anxieties—about school, popularity, abilities, strangers, anything at all—will be someone who can express "deep" emotions and understand hers.

The ability to take a friend's perspective and make an effort to sympathize regardless of their own feelings is an example of the greater maturity of eight-to-ten-year-olds' friendships. Many children of this age will say their "real" friends are people who listen and don't judge you. The children's social styles become increasingly less important as they develop other qualities—compassion, tact, concern, and so on—that they can share with one another.

Kids at this age are also more at ease with their internal policeman. For example, just because Andrea thinks it's not cool to hang out in the bank parking lot with the teenagers after school doesn't mean she will stop playing with Betty because she does it.

Yet, paradoxically, children of this age will agonize over a friend's upsetting behavior. A Follower who was told by his Naysayer friend that the boy had put a kitten in a pail and tried to drown it but stopped before the animal died was enormously anxious about what he should have done. Should he have "told"? Should he counsel his friend by himself? Should he suggest that the friend tell his parents or the school counselor? This morass of new moral and emotional issues can be very difficult for the eight-to-ten-year-old to handle alone—which is why having a best friend to share it with can be so vital.

A Boss or a Strong-Willed Child might handle difficult times with action instead of words, for example, by rescuing another kid who was being roughed up by a bully. A Thinker or a Shy Child might not trust another as much as she trusts herself. As one nine-year-old put it when her mother suggested that she wouldn't feel so alone if she talked out a problem with a friend, "It doesn't really matter if I'm alone or not alone, this is what I'm dealing with right now." This child relies on her inner resources to deal with problems. She doesn't like the idea that friendship might be used in order to get approval or corroboration of her feelings, which she is pretty sure about all on her own.

Your Child/Your Role

HAS YOUR CHILD EVER:

- Come home furious because a new friend "just didn't understand"?
- Listened closely to a friend's problem, then come up with a totally inappropriate solution?
- Reacted in a way you consider tactless, for example, laughing when a sad story is told?

Part of growing up is learning to use the abstract qualities that seem so ephemeral when we try to pin them down. You want your child to feel for others when the situation warrants it. You want to encourage the social skills of waiting and observing, showing empathy and consideration, and finding solutions. However, you don't want your child to bare his soul only to be rejected by a friend who's not capable of handling this level of emotionality.

You might want to explain to your child that some kids are amenable to "deep talk" and others prefer to keep things on the surface. You could suggest that if he's not sure about his relationship with a particular child, he can test the waters by giving out some less serious information before confiding something secret and special. In our earlier example Ralph now knows that Frank could be trusted with any worries he might have about switching schools next year, but he may not be completely confident yet that Frank is the kind of guy he could talk to about his parents' divorce. He may need a few other in-depth conversations to figure out just how much trust to put in this new friend. Very often a child will have to try reaching out and get rebuffed in order to learn this hard lesson.

A child who has some of the emotional abilities for forming close friendships may still be confused as to how to use them. He may joke around and toss off a "funny story" when he's really trying to find a way to share a confidence. The kid who laughs and says, "Boy, you should have seen my little brother wheezing last night. He turned this fantastic shade of blue!" may be revealing his intense concern about his brother's chronic asthma condition. This child is showing his cards, but upside down, and your child may not get it and think his friend is acting crass and mean. Friendship dilemmas may result because of these crossed emotional circuits.

This misinterpretation of mood is very understandable. You can work with your child by listening to TV or real-life situations and asking, "What did you think he really meant when he said that?" By encouraging your child to think for a moment before reacting, you'll be able to get him more on target with emotional exchanges. (See the "Social Skills Verbal Kit, Section 1. Find the Hidden Emotion," page 152.)

It's very common at this age for supremely confident children to go through an anxious phase as they begin to sense these deeper emotional issues coming to the fore. The Boss or Strong-Willed Child who always separated from you easily may now cry for a couple of nights before going away to sleep-over camp. Your former Adapter who could shrug off any troubles may now have a host of unexplainable fears. Don't belittle his concerns or try to make them go away. This can be an excellent preparation for dealing with even bigger challenges later on. It's better for a child to come to terms with his vulnerability now than when he leaves home for college or gets his first job.

You can help by listening to him as he sorts through his feelings. Listening *well* to your child reduces his anxiety and facilitiates his own, independent problem-solving abilities. When he knows he has your ear and the time to think through concerns, he'll be better able to come up with his own solutions. The "Peer Pressure Puzzles" and "Looking In from the Other Side" questions in this chapter and the next will allow you to explore some of these difficult emotional areas together with your child. Remember to keep your own fears and anxieties in check as you listen—don't add to his worries by piling your own on top.

You might want to suggest that he share his concerns with a couple of his closest friends. When he is able to see that his pals are going through similar experiences, he will feel less alone. Also, his friends' ideas about what to do may be significantly different—and maybe even more relevant—than yours.

VIOLATION OF TRUST:
"I'll never speak to Janie again— she kept a secret from me."

Janie, an eight-and-a-half-year-old Follower who could also be an Adapter, always saved a seat on the school bus for Maggi, a Performer and Strong-Willed Child.

When Janie was paired up with Dorothy to write a special tribute to a teacher, Maggi began feeling very left out. The next afternoon, when she got on the bus to go home and walked to the back to take her seat, Dorothy was already in it.

Maggi stared at Janie. "I always sit there," she said.

"Sorry, but we need to work on our song for Mrs. Burd," Dorothy said. Maggi started to take the seat in the next row, but Janie stuck her book bag in it. "This is secret," she said. "We need some privacy, please."

Maggi told her mother that afternoon that she would never speak to Janie again. "I can't believe what an awful person she is," she told her mom.

Her mother tried to reason with her, saying that if the song was in fact supposed to be a surprise for the class, then it was kind of understandable that Maggi would be excluded.

"Come on, sweetheart, give her another chance," her mother said.

"She blew it," Maggi stated flatly.

What's Really Going On?

Maggi is responding to the fact that Janie broke several of the girls' unspoken rules: We always sit together, we always share information, and we don't go outside the relationship for intimacies. Maggi feels betrayed by the fact that she gave her trust to this friend who broke it.

The girls are, however, working from two different premises. Maggi sees a continuity in their relationship and wants an exclusivity. Janie, on the other hand, feels like Maggi is a good friend but perhaps not a best friend. She didn't give that much thought to letting a special school project come between her and Maggi.

When two children come to a friendship with two different sets of expectations, feelings are bound to be hurt. The question, depending on the child's social style and level of maturity, is, Will this incident resolve itself, or is it the beginning of the end? As Maggi put it, did her friend "blow it"?

For the friendship to continue, both girls may need to evolve. Janie may need to realize that her remarks were hurtful and learn to assert herself more tactfully. Maggi may need to accept less exclusivity and learn the distinction between good and best friends. However, even best friends will have needs and activities outside their best friendship.

Your Child/Your Role

HAS YOUR CHILD EVER:

- Come home in tears because another kid copied his homework?
- Assured you that he would never speak to his best friend again because the friend had told another kid something that was supposed to be confidential?
- Seemed depressed because one child or a group of children had promised something and then not delivered it?
- Insisted that his friend swear a "blood oath" or perform some serious ritual involving lifelong commitment?

We live in an imperfect world, and it is our job as parents to assuage the hurts and try to make our children understand the principles of compromise and second chances.

One way we can do this is to model trusting and forgiving behavior. If you keep the secret that your child told you, and if you don't hold a grudge against your partner for forgetting to mail your urgent package, you are giving your child the message that friends can do good things *and* bad things and can get mad and then make up and still be friends.

Once again your role as a parent is to listen well. This means setting aside a special time to be your child's sounding board—without being interrupted by siblings, phone calls, or other disturbances. If your child is going through a rocky period socially, make sure your partner, a grandparent, or a sitter is around to be with your other children so that you can devote some special time to the child who needs help.

Try to recall some friendship problems that you might have had at your child's age. Your child will be comforted to realize that you shared the same kinds of struggles. This will make you less of an authority figure and more of a human being who has weaknesses too. By perceiving the similarities between you, your child will be better able to rally her self-esteem. She'll see that she can't be "bad" or a failure if the same thing happened to Mom!

Showing empathy to your child is another way to validate her feelings. If you say, "You must have been so hurt when Gail ignored you!" she knows it's okay for her to be angry at Gail and to want to let off steam. If she's in distress about the behavior of a very good friend, you might want to encourage her to talk to the other child about the incident so that they can work it through together. This will also give her the opportunity to see whether Gail is a friend worth keeping. Use your Social Skills Verbal Kit together to work on hidden emotions and peer pressure, and check ahead to the next chapter for the exercise on mutual perspective taking.

If your child is in a situation where *he* has violated the trust of a friend, and that friend is upset enough not to accept phone calls or playdates, you owe it to your child to have a serious discussion about trust. Your eight-to-ten-year-old is now sophisticated enough to understand the question, How would you feel if he did it to you? Sorting through the answers gives a child of any social style a chance to find resolutions. (See "Developing Your Child's Empathy," Chapter Six, and "Looking In from the Other Side," Chapter Eight.)

Your child must first acknowledge that something he did sparked a pal's anger. This is sometimes hard for kids who strongly defend their egos and their actions. The best approach is to avoid blaming and judging, trying instead to get him to tell you all the events in order so that you can make sense of them together. He may be less defensive if you tell him about a mistake you made—and acknowledged— with a friend. You might try asking what else your child could have done in the situation, in order to figure out together why he acted as he did and how he could make the situation better.

You may discover in the course of this talk that the biggest stumbling block to reconciliation is the *other* child's grudge. Your child will have to be open-minded enough to confront and overcome that hostility—if he chooses to—with a heartfelt apology. It's hard to say, "I'm really sorry," and mean it, but if the other person accepts the apology well, the rewards can be extraordinary. If the apology isn't accepted, you will naturally want to help your child deal with his hurt feelings by listening and sympathizing. You can also praise his maturity in being able to offer the apology in the first place. But your intervention may do nothing to ease the pain of the breakup. Disappointments and cruelties are part of life, and they hurt whether we're nine or fifty-nine.

If a friend gets your child into trouble at school or on a team because of a violation of trust, it may be necessary for you to take direct action. For example, if your daughter's seat mate copied her writing assignment and your child is the one accused of plagiarism, you may have to talk with the teacher about separating the two children.

It's not a good idea to step in to settle any kind of trust violation unless your child knows what you're doing and why. As you'll see in the next section, this is an age when kids want to find answers on their own, without much parental intervention. They may not know exactly how to fix a problem, but you have to let them try. You'll also have to let them get hurt every once in a while as they discover their own blend of temperateness and assertiveness.

You must remember, too, never to violate your child's trust. You've got to be a good role model. As your child's primary moral influence, you owe it to her to stand by your beliefs and ethics. This doesn't mean you should have knee-jerk reactions to all moral issues, but you should be consistent. If you're outraged about a political campaign that downplays the importance of minority rights, for example, but then you discriminate in your private life, you are sending a very mixed message to your child.

SEPARATION FROM PARENTS:
"We worked it out ourselves, without you, Mom."

Sean's mother was worried when Richard's mother drove nine-year-old Sean home before the end of their playdate. "I don't think our children play very well together," Richard's mother said tightly. She was holding the pieces of an expensive china bowl.

Sean's mother demanded to know what had happened and even offered to pay for the bowl if her son was responsible, but Richard's mother said that no money was necessary.

"The boys wouldn't tell me how it happened, and your son was very arrogant when I demanded to know who did it," she said. "I just don't think Sean is a good influence on my child," she persisted.

Sean's mother respected her Thinker son's silence, but a week later, noticing that he was still very moody, she did say, "I'd like to clear up the whole mess about the broken bowl. Why don't you tell me what happened?"

"Richard's mom would *kill* him. I can't," Sean said.

Sean's mother could see how upset he was, and offered to call Richard's mother and figure out some way to make everyone blameless, but Sean shook his head. "I can handle it, Mom," he said stoically. "It wouldn't be cool for Richard."

What's Really Going On?

Sean doesn't blame his friend Richard, even though he's being blamed for Richard's accident. Was it really Richard's fault that the bowl broke? We'll never know. The point is that the two boys, who are good friends, honor and respect each other's silence. The only important element for Sean is that his mother not run interference for him. Even though it means that he will be deprived of playing with someone he really likes, he will not be a mama's boy. He can't even consider setting the facts straight with Richard's mother so that he can pursue his relationship with Richard.

Sean doesn't want to tamper with his friend's relationship with his family, and this shows an enormous sophistication on his part. When he says, "It wouldn't be cool for Richard," he is speaking about the incident from his friend's perspective, *even though* he knows it means that Richard's family's will continue to blame him and prevent him from seeing his friend. He has grasped two very important elements here that will serve him well for the rest of his life: It wasn't fair and it wasn't his fault, but because he now sees himself as an individual and not just a kid in a family, he cannot allow his mother to fix things for him.

Sean also has a perspective on Richard's relationship with his mother. He sees that Richard can't go to bat for him because he might be severely punished and might also lose the confidence of his overly strict mother. The multiple points of view involved here are tenuously balanced. Both boys accept the unfortunate realities of the situation.

With younger boys, this scene would never have happened. Younger children don't yet have this great sense of allegiance to friends, because they are still basically family oriented. In addition young children are far too egocentric to take the rap for something they didn't do.

Your Child/Your Role

HAS YOUR CHILD EVER:

- Been furious with you when you made a phone call to arrange a playdate?
- Refused to let you in her room or demanded a lock on her door?
- Suddenly stopped confiding in you?
- Started talking back or been brutally honest to the point of hurting your feelings?

Separation from your children is never easy, whether they're two or twenty. But when your children begin to separate from you, which is a natural thing for them to do from eight to ten, it can be heartrending.

One mother reported that her Team Player and Adapter, who had gone off to summer camp, didn't greet her with open arms on his return. "I didn't miss you a bit," he told her frankly, "even though Dad told me to tell you I did." The boy had no idea that his mother might be hurt by this announcement. This was his own blunt way of celebrating his newfound independence.

Some extroverted children have a lot of trouble at this stage sorting out anger from independence. A child who suddenly begins lashing out is trying hard to go it on his own. In your own way you must stand up for your rights as well as do some soul-searching on the subject of how overly protective or demanding you might be. It can be helpful to tell your child that your feelings count just as much as his friends'. If he's tactful and concerned about hurting his pals, he should extend the same consideration to you. In the example above, the mother told her son that although she was delighted he'd done so well at camp, it would be nice for him to think about the way he said things to her, because her feelings counted as well.

Of course there are also children who don't feel comfortable making the break at this time. They want to feel grown up, yet they cherish the protection of their parents, which they rightly sense is becoming less central in their lives. You may note some regressive behavior—baby talk or clinginess—that you haven't seen for a couple of years. Your child is trying to tell you that she needs you, and your best response is to ignore the childish behavior and be supportive and encouraging about all the new, independent things she is doing.

As your child matures, you will be most helpful to him if you can blend your empathic and firm-guiding qualities. There will be times when your child is upset about something and needs you to be understanding; there will be other times when only a direct, no-nonsense attitude will get him out of his mood. As you experiment in each situation to see what works, you'll begin to feel instinctively when you should be close and cuddly and when you should stand back and encourage your child's independence.

You also must accept that there will be times when nothing you can do will make much difference. Part of maturing is accepting that things are not perfect and that when we're upset, we cannot always be comforted or comfort ourselves— at least not right away.

When your child is under stress, knowing her unique blend of social skills will help you to coax her out of a depressed mood more easily. You can persuade a Team Player who becomes a Strong-Willed Child when upset to reflect a little on his situation. Then you might suggest that he go out and throw a ball or run around the block, just to blow off steam. You can get a Thinker who tends to fall into the Fragile Flower category when she feels down to lose herself in a book or a CD she particularly likes.

The best thing you can do is convince your eight-to-ten-year-old to believe in her own inner resources. When you support your child's confidence in her social intelligence and can help to enhance it, you are giving the most precious gift of all.

WARNING SIGNS THAT YOUR CHILD MIGHT NEED HELP

As your child experiments with new skills at this time of life, her friendships may not always proceed smoothly. You may be concerned about behavior that seems different or trouble-some. Some new abilities are mastered very slowly, but if you notice that your child is having real problems consistently with the issues in this chapter, consult Chapter Nine, "Children Who Can't Reach Out."

Ask yourself the following questions about your child. If the answer to several of the items is affirmative *on a regular basis*, your child may need professional help:

- Does your child always need to get his own way, regardless of another child's feelings?
- Has your child begun to emulate another child in ways that seem completely unlike his own personality?
- Has your child selected one exclusive friend who is intimidating and bullying him?
- Does your child seem unable to exhibit appropriate emotional reactions—that is, does he laugh when told about something sad or unpleasant?
- Does your child seem terribly depressed or anxious, particularly about handling new situations?

• Is your child acting so rebellious toward you that you feel that you are constantly disciplining him?

With the information you now have about your child's friendships from eight to ten years of age, you can encourage the more complex social skills of preadolescence. By stepping back and allowing your child to make some mistakes and claim his own rewards in social settings, you are offering the best parenting help possible.

8

FRIENDSHIP AMONG CHILDREN AGES TEN TO TWELVE

"Gee, Mom, why are you so mad? Janice's dad said he'd drive us to the mall at three, and I forgot Aunt Barbara was coming over with her new baby. Is it really such a big deal that I missed her?" asks eleven-year-old Angela with a shrug. You wonder, is this your problem or hers? Lately the family simply doesn't seem to matter to Angela.

"Chuck says Joe was really burned about my quitting the team. It didn't matter to him that I was doing it because I have to pull my grades up—I should have remembered how much stake he puts in loyalty to the team," ten-year-old George said solemnly. His father was impressed that George could see so many sides to this problem at once.

"Look, I'm meeting someone at the library. That's all I can say." Paul, who'd just turned twelve, couldn't even look at the other guys as he walked away quickly. They all knew, because they felt it themselves: If you were meeting a girl, you didn't talk about it.

183

WHAT MAKES PARENTS ANXIOUS?

It's finally happened. Your baby is not a baby anymore. This person, who may be almost up to your shoulder or may even be able to look you straight in the eye (when he feels like it!), is straddling the bridge between childhood and young adulthood. Friendships at this stage now really resemble our own relationships with friends—with the exception that we have a lot more practice at bonding, coming unstuck, and meeting up again. Our children are just in the training stage of this exciting and difficult process.

There will naturally be many hurts and hardships along the path. Preadolescents' varying facility with social skills can confuse the most tolerant parent.

It can be difficult, for instance, to feel that you are no longer always the person your child wants to confide in. Friends may have usurped your importance in your child's life—at least for the time being. If you are patient, and if you can swallow your own longing to be the primary nurturer *all* the time, your child will come to you when it really counts.

It is also tough for many parents to know where to draw the line on setting limits at this age. If you forbid your child to participate in activities that his peers are "into" right now, you may be propelling him headlong into very rebellious behavior in a few short years. You know you can't say no to everything, but how do you determine when to say yes? Kids are exposed to so many things they aren't emotionally ready to experience. For this reason they desperately need to be reined in, particularly in situations that may be potentially dangerous, either physically or emotionally.

WHAT ISSUES ARE PARAMOUNT
FOR YOUR CHILD RIGHT NOW?

The main friendship issues for this age group are the following:

- Mutual perspective taking, which includes the cognitive and emotional awareness of one or several other people
- Conflict of family needs versus friends' needs
- Beginning opposite-sex bonding
- Peer pressure

Children in the ten-to-twelve age group are now able to step out of the self-centered two-party system of thinking and feeling and make the leap to *mutual perspective taking*. This is known as *recursive* thinking, an ability to think about what another person is thinking. (This is not the same as empathy, which is the ability to *feel* the emotions that another person feels in a particular situation.) According to Dr. Robert L. Selman, a professor of education and psychiatry at Harvard University, the ability to see things from someone else's point of view is a real indicator of maturity in interpersonal relationships. The preadolescent can stand outside her own opinions, fears, and hopes and view not just herself vis-à-vis another friend, but herself *plus* that friend as seen from a third party's perspective.

Recursive thinking allows an older child to understand and forgive a friend for infractions that would have infuriated a younger child. Whereas the eight-to-ten-year-old usually stands his ground about being right in an important argument, the ten-to-twelve-year-old can acknowledge that someone else could in fact be just as right or even "righter" than he is—at least some of the time.

The conflict of family versus friends that begins during ages eight to ten and continues through adolescence can be a

185

shocker, especially if you've always had a close relationship with your child. Your preadolescent may tell you some of what's going on in his life, but not everything. He may change a story to protect himself or a pal. There may be certain subjects he feels more comfortable talking about to a best friend. But he will always want to know that you are there for him if he needs an anchor.

Bonding with the opposite sex is a logical extension of having a same-sex "chum." The empathy that your child developed is now firmly established, and he or she is ready to seek out friendships with those who are different—even in gender. Naturally, developmental changes that occur at this time affect personality. As preadolescent hormones make voices deepen and breasts bud, there is a concurrent new interest in the "romantic" aspects of friendship. This causes—as we can all recall—a sometimes paralyzing self-consciousness and embarrassment about physical and emotional changes.

Peer-group pressure is an enormous influence on children in this age group, and it affects different children in different ways. The ten-to-twelve-year-old is constantly feeling the need for greater self-definition as he turns away from purely family-centered activities.

You will remember the earlier stage of this developmental phenomenon from Chapter Four, where toddlers first experience their identity as separate and apart from that of the parent. Now, in preadolescence, these feelings are deeper, and the struggle for independence is often a battle fiercely fought. But the preadolescent, feeling that it's too soon and too scary really to be out on his own, at least has an option the two-year-old never had: For the older child the peer group becomes the new home base. This has drawbacks as well as advantages—depending on the dynamics, the group can stifle self-definition just as readily as the family ever did. But a child whose family encouraged self-confidence way back in the toddler years has a much better chance of holding up against the group's pressure now.

The preteen peer group allows for lots of practice in consolidating *interlocking friendships* and developing social skills independent of parental judgment or support. Dealing with more than one friend at the same time lets us see many points of view at once. It's possible that if we never bond with a group, the skills we need to help us negotiate and resolve conflicts in work or family may develop more slowly or not at all. The time from ten-to-twelve is typically one where a child makes the transition from one-on-one intimacy to working well in a group setting.

MUTUAL PERSPECTIVE TAKING:
"Melanie's sister got sick because we kept her up."

Sue, a Performer and occasional Naysayer, was best friends with Melanie, a Fragile Flower and Thinker. They had been having sleep-overs for several years, and their families considered these eleven-year-old children to be as close as sisters.

On one particular occasion when Sue stayed over at Melanie's house, they decided they would stay up all night. Melanie's older sister, Roberta, told them before she went to bed that she felt like she was coming down with a cold. She had planned to study for the SATs with a friend the next day, so she wanted to feel rested the next morning.

Melanie and Sue spent the night talking, listening to CDs, doing their nails and hair, and so on. Roberta asked them to pipe down a couple of times, and they'd be quiet for a while until their giggles got the best of them. The next morning, rather groggy, the group appeared at the breakfast table.

Roberta was coughing and blowing her nose.

"You don't look so great," Melanie told her.

"I don't feel so great. I didn't get any sleep."

Melanie shrugged. "Too bad."

"It was all your fault," Roberta said. "You guys are so inconsiderate, I can't believe you. I *told* you I needed a quiet night." She took the box of tissues off the table and left in a huff.

"Oh, boy," Melanie said glumly. "She's in a *great* mood."

Sue looked at her nails. "Geez, I guess we blew it. I never thought we were that loud, but we really kept her up. You think we should apologize?"

What's Really Going On?

Children of this age have their own agenda. Melanie and Sue had made a pact to stay up, and they completed their mission.

But both girls are eventually able to see Roberta's perspective as well as their own. Although it didn't occur to them at the time that they were disturbing her, when they saw the next morning how their partying had affected her, they were immediately sorry. They can stand back and see Roberta's foul mood as legitimate.

Sue has always been something of a Naysayer and is used to putting her back up when crossed. Now, however, she is able to empathize with Roberta.

A child who has always been a Team Player will probably have the quickest adaptation to this friendship skill, but this concept can be difficult to grasp for the ten-to-twelve-year-old who excels at getting his own point across. If Sue had been a Boss or a Strong-Willed Child, she might have denied that what she'd done had affected Roberta's health. Instead she respected the older girl's feelings and was willing to apologize for her actions.

Introverted children like Melanie need to strike a balance between the different perspectives in a situation like this, because the extreme self-consciousness of many Fragile Flowers, Thinkers, and Shy Children of this age group can make recursive thinking almost painful at times. They may focus so hard on others' perspectives that they become very self-effacing or self-critical. (This can cause problems with peer pressure, as we'll see in a minute.)

Your Child/Your Role

HAS YOUR CHILD EVER:

- Pointed out some behavior of yours as inappropriate because of the way it might affect another person?
- Acted as negotiator for two other friends?
- Forgiven a friend or group of friends for something they've done because "they had their own reasons"?
- Gotten into a debate with a friend about some cause —either social, environmental, or political—and completely switched sides halfway through the argument?

Your child may suddenly develop a very caustic tongue, enjoying the role of third-party observer. This may boomerang on you as your son or daughter begins to critique your every move and decision. Understand that you are not the target—your child is testing her newfound skill of standing in several different pairs of shoes at one time.

Conversely there may be times when you are maddened by your child's apparent indecisiveness. Why can't he make up his mind? It's not that he has no mind of his own or is just being "wise." It's more like a playful shifting of gears, which will eventually come to rest in one position or another in adolescence.

A child who successfully balances these two extremes can develop some exceptionally advanced social skills as a negotiator. The ability to set aside her own wants and needs can open a child up to the possibility that others have their own reasons for doing things. A ten-to-twelve-year-old who can see this has a rich social future ahead.

How You Can Encourage Appropriate Social Skills

The poet Robert Burns wrote, "Oh wad some power the giftie gie us / To see oursels as others see us!" There are many adults who lack this gift, and it sorely interferes with their interactions with others in work situations and in love relationships. So it's important to support this sophisticated form of thinking when you see it in your child. You can do this by taking *his* perspective, thereby modeling how one person can "try on" another's feelings. Or you can ask what he thinks *your* perspective is in any given conflict. If he thinks first about what motivates you and your partner, he will get practice looking outside while he looks inside.

During your daily catching-up time with your child, you can use the mutual-perspective exercises that follow. Allow your child to make up a few scenarios of his own. By using your imagination and conjuring up possibilities for the way others feel, you'll help your child cultivate this essential social skill.

LOOKING IN FROM THE OTHER SIDE: TAKING MUTUAL PERSPECTIVES

The ability to think about what another person is thinking is a very adult friendship skill. When your child can do this he opens himself to a wider worldview.

The examples below will give you a good start on mutual perspective taking with your preadolescent child. You may want to return to them at different times as your child gradually deepens his thinking on these issues.

1. Ken's brother, Theo, tells him that he overheard Ken and his friend Bob planning to play a practical joke on him. What was Theo's reaction to learning what his brother intended to do?

2. Sophia and Maureen are caught shoplifting some makeup in a local store. How do their parents feel when they are told what happened?

3. Pam discovers that Clark let Tony copy from his test, right after he gave her a big song and dance about honesty. What does Pam think of Clark?

4. Jeannie's sister, Lois, tells her that she overheard Jeannie telling her friend how lonely she felt last weekend with just her family around. How does Lois feel about what her sister said?

5. You and a friend are talking together after school, and a third boy, who happens to be short, walks by. Your friend yells, "See you later, shrimp!" How do you think the boy feels?

6. You and your best friend get together with a third girl, Jana. You remember a secret you wanted to tell your best friend and start whispering to her in front of Jana. How does Jana feel?

7. Alan and his pal Bill are part of a youth group. As a special treat their counselor takes them out for pizza after the meeting. The boys start talking loudly, play with their food,

and unscrew the tops of the salt-and-pepper shakers. The waiter complains. How does their counselor feel?

8. Your friend persuades you to borrow a sweater that belongs to her older sister. You spill cranberry juice on it, but when you return it, you don't mention the accident. How does your friend's sister feel when she discovers it later? How does your friend feel about your not telling her?

9. Your divorced father has started dating a new woman whom you don't particularly like. You are complaining about her on the phone to your friend when you realize she's walked into the next room and has probably heard everything you said. How do you think she feels?

10. Your friend's team just lost the last game of the season, and your team won. You're careful not to brag when you're alone with your friend, but when the whole group gets together, you hoot and holler about how great your team is. How do you think the members of his team feel?

CONFLICT BETWEEN FAMILY AND FRIENDS:
"I had to be with my friends, Dad—I can see you anytime."

Michael, at eleven, had always been a Follower and a Thinker. He was much more family-oriented than his nine-year-old brother, Joey. While Joey went to sleep-away camp one summer, Michael stayed home and got friendly with "the guys" who hung out at the town pool. One of the boys he really got to like was Brendan. Brendan was twelve and a half, a Team Player and Adapter, and because of his independence he was generally a good influence on Michael.

Michael's family traditionally watched the end of the World Series together, preparing a meal that they ate in front of the TV. On the afternoon of the party, however, Michael suddenly announced to his mom that he wouldn't be around because he and Brendan had made plans. He was gone by the time his father got home from the office. When Brendan's parents brought Michael back after the game was over, Michael's father was kind of moody.

"Hey, didn't your team win?" Michael teased his father, and got no reponse. His mother said quietly, "It was really more important for Michael to be with his buddies this year, don't you agree?" Michael's dad reluctantly acknowledged that it was okay for Michael to be off with Brendan and his friends.

Later Michael's mom asked Michael to apologize for the way he'd handled the situation. He shrugged as he approached his father. "Gee, Dad, I'm sorry if I hurt your feelings, but I *had* to be with the guys. I can see you anytime."

What's Really Going On?

Michael did hurt his father's feelings, and he's aware of what he did, yet the pull toward solidarity with a group conflicts with his family allegiance. It's taken Michael a considerable amount of time to feel as independent as his brother does, and the difficulty he's having with separation makes him awkward in dealing with his father's feelings. Consequently he had to work hard to prepare himself for *not* doing an activity with his father that he's done for years. First he watched his younger brother go off to camp. Then he met Brendan and his buddies at the pool. They were older and had more practice in being independent and on their own. Michael was learning by emulating their behavior.

In the meantime his father was having his own separation problems. He seems taken aback by Michael's decision to watch the game with his friends. It would be useful for Michael's parents to sit down with him and talk about how the family is handling his newfound independence. This would give Michael the opportunity to do some work on mutual perspective taking (see box on page 191). If he had been more attuned to his father's feelings, for example, he might have called him midway through the game to get an update on the score, or written his dad a note before leaving the house.

Your Child/Your Role

HAS YOUR CHILD EVER:

- Promised to come with you on an outing, then neglected to show up without even calling?
- Been particularly caustic about the personalities of different family members?
- Taunted a younger sibling about his attachment to family?

Some families value closeness so highly that the breakaway is delayed until their child reaches adolescence—or even later. But parents of most ten-to-twelve-year-olds will see an inevitable switch from faithful participation in family-centered events to a desire for more activity with friends.

It's not always easy to watch your child make this change at eleven or twelve. Although he used to love visits with Aunt Mary and Uncle Joe, now the mere mention of their names may result in complaining, sulking, or just not appearing when they come over. You may note an attitude problem about anything relating to family. It's possible that your usually helpful child will suddenly refuse to do family chores or give you high-level resistance about taking care of a younger sibling. It's important that you not take this behavior personally; on the other hand, you do have to set limits that will give your child *permissible* parameters for striking out on his own.

Children who have a lot of trouble splitting their loyalties will claim that they want independence, but then will barrage their parents with little decisions such as what shirt to wear in the morning. A typical situation might be a Shy Child who agrees to walk the neighbor's dog after school but keeps falling down on the job, forgetting or arriving late, then asking his parent to patch up what he's done wrong. Here is an instance where a child should be allowed to make mistakes and correct them himself.

How You Can Encourage
Appropriate Social Skills

It's important to encourage leadership of course, but children of this age should also be aware that they cannot disregard family responsibilities. They must learn to use the social skills of finding solutions and making peace. And for their own safety they will have to learn to follow rules that you will establish *with* them. You will have to sit down with your child and figure out a good working plan so that family events don't turn into repeated clashes of wills. For example, you may wish to state that Thanksgiving this year is just for you and your relatives, but allow your child to invite a friend and his family over the day after. Over the weekend when the grandparents visit from New Hampshire, you might allow him to choose a four-hour segment when he can be with friends.

This is a good time to establish more adult-type responsibilities for your independence-craving eleven- or twelve-year-old. Suppose you offer to pay him a salary for watching a sibling for a couple of hours when you're out of the house or need to get some work done. Part of this job could involve helping his younger brother or sister with his or her homework. Or you might decide together that one night a week he gets to help prepare dinner. Learning to cook or care for a young child will give him both a sense of independence from you and a sense of competence about his ability to handle real-life events on his own.

If your child knows he's supposed to be home before dark, but he calls to ask permission to stay at his pal's house— even when he knows you have dinner waiting on the table— allow him some flexibility. You can compromise: He must come home for dinner with the family, but afterward you'll drive him back to the friend's house for the evening. This way he has to delay his gratification, but gets to spend time with both family and friends.

Let your child know that he must *always* touch base with you on important issues and that you expect prior notification if he has an "emergency" that prevents him from getting home in time for a family event. (Be sure to define what you consider to be an emergency.)

If your child should break some previously established rules, don't humiliate him in front of a friend, even if you're really angry. There will be time afterward for you two to discuss in private what he's done. It's crucial that he have the chance to save face with his peers.

Parents who are Firm Guiders will see the best results on this issue. If you play Tough Guy and insist that he join in the fun time you've planned, it won't be fun for anyone. You may also set up future antagonism between you. Walk a middle line: Help your child make some decisions, and bolster her self-worth by letting her make others by herself. If she makes the wrong decisions, she'll learn by doing.

Always assure your child that you're here for her, available for advice and counsel. The mutual-perspectives examples (see box on page 191) will get your child to think more about what you and others might feel in a given situation. They will also allow you to see things from her point of view as well.

OPPOSITE-SEX INTIMACY:
*"She's not my girlfriend;
she's just a friend."*

Carl was really upset when his best friend, Pete, moved across the country. Both boys, at twelve, were Adapters and Thinkers, and although Pete had a mild learning disorder and Carl was in several G&T (Gifted and Talented) classes, the apparent differences in their academic capacity vanished when the boys were together.

When Pete left, Carl didn't want to hang out with any other boy. Most of the kids he knew were gung-ho for sports, while Carl enjoyed playing in the school orchestra. After practice one day he noticed that Cheryl, a Strong-Willed Performer, was walking toward his street. He caught up with her, and she told him that she'd just moved to a house near his. "Why don't we walk to school together tomorrow?" he suggested.

The trip to and from school became a daily event. Carl didn't mention to his parents that he was walking with Cheryl, but his mother knew that if Carl didn't get home exactly on time, she could find him at Cheryl's. One day she found them sitting in her kitchen when she walked in from grocery shopping. They seemed embarrassed, but neither made any attempt to end their conversation.

Carl didn't feel a "boy-girl" attraction to Cheryl so much as the desire to be friends with someone good to talk to. He discussed things with Cheryl that were different from what he had discussed with Pete. Sometimes Carl and Cheryl would talk about really serious issues, such as "What is *empty*? What is *nothing*?" and sometimes they acted silly together. Mostly they enjoyed being in the orchestra, going to concerts, and just hanging out together. Carl felt he could trust Cheryl with his most secret thoughts. He'd never felt so deeply about a friend before.

197

What's Really Going On?

Carl didn't "replace" Pete with Cheryl. But Pete happened to leave town at just the right time, developmentally, for Carl to select a girl as his next confidante. The other boys he'd spent time with were "jocks," who weren't at all interested in the kind of intellectual and emotional exploration typical of girls of this age. Carl, on the other hand, was really in sync with Cheryl's interests. She also didn't laugh at him when he came up with a heavy philosophical question.

A twelve-year-old's self-image is sometimes clearer when it is reflected by someone quite different from his or her same-sex friends.

Simultaneous with emotional development at this age, of course, is physical development. Carl and Cheryl are both going through hormonal changes that bring sex back from its hideout during the middle childhood years (usually from about ages seven to eleven). The warmth and comfort of talking to a girl coincides with the new physical pull of Carl's energies toward a member of the opposite sex. Although preadolescents are embarrassed by their unpredictable bodies and wildly fluctuating emotions, they are still eager to try out their new status as "man" and "woman."

This is not to imply that they are in any way ready to engage in sexual relationships. Most children of this age don't immediately associate bonding with the opposite sex with sexual behavior. They may hold hands and kiss their opposite-sex pal occasionally, but this is not generally the focus of the relationship.

It is vital, however, that you pay attention to your child's relative naïveté about sexual matters. If your child has locked the door on you, he may simply want privacy to read or listen to music or think. He or she may also be experimenting with masturbation and sex play. It is essential, in this age of sexually transmitted diseases and behavioral atrocities such as date rape, that your child is protected with the vital facts.

You certainly should find out what your child's school is teaching in its Family Life Education courses, and whenever the occasion arises, make your child aware of the profound responsibilities that sexual behavior entails. This includes a discussion with boys and girls about contraception, pregnancy, sexually transmitted diseases—including HIV and AIDS—and the emotional upheaval that early sexual activity can cause.

In our society it is more than common to find that over-stimulated children with too much freedom begin to experiment with behaviors that can lead to serious problems. It's hard enough to deal with the confusion and turmoil of the teen years without the additional trauma of an unwanted pregnancy or STD. Preadolescents should be given definite limits on their private time together so that they won't feel compelled to act out sexually.

The extroverts in our chart (boys and girls both) can handle opposite-sex relationships more easily than the introverts, specifically because of their predilection for enthusiasm and fun. They won't take every missed phone call from a boyfriend or girlfriend as a personal slight and will be able to tolerate some teasing from members of their same-sex group.

Introverted children, however, particularly boys, may not show any interest in the opposite sex. But the seeds of this interest are there, waiting to blossom later, when children have a little more self-confidence.

Boys tend to lag behind girls in their interest in opposite-sex relationships. Their physical maturation tends to occur later than girls', as does their facility with sophisticated social skills. Naturally, however, there are exceptions to every rule, and many boys of twelve are just as capable as girls of taking mutual perspectives and understanding the feelings of someone quite different from themselves.

Your Child/Your Role

HAS YOUR CHILD EVER:

• Disappeared for an afternoon and been absolutely silent (even when you threaten to discipline him) about where he's been?
• Insisted on bringing what you might consider an inappropriate gift to an opposite-sex friend?
• Locked his door and refused to let you in?
• Said really terrible things about a member of the opposite sex in public, although you know they have been seeing each other as a couple?

This is an area where parents are often shut out. Your ten-to-twelve-year-old's new interest in the opposite sex may be too embarrassing to discuss with mom and dad—so don't push it!

Preadolescent children bond with a friend who can help them feel their own maleness or femaleness. It makes a girl feel good about herself when a boy takes her seriously and enjoys talking with her. It makes a boy feel a sense of worth when he can leave the locker-room banter of his same-sex pals and explore the depths of his personality with a girl.

In preadolescence a girl may be concerned about what boys think of her looks and behaviors, but she has not yet developed the self-consciousness of the teen years. The anxiety about pleasing the opposite sex stifles many teenage girls' ability to be honest or comfortable about their dealings with boys. But from age ten-to-twelve, girls are usually free to accept complex relationships with same- and opposite-sex friends and to explore all the many facets of themselves: tomboy, dreamer, brain, and mischief maker.

Boys of this age may need to act "macho" to prove themselves, but, as with girls, they are still able to be both vulnerable and childlike as well as brave and "masculine." They are not yet fixed in their conviction that they have to behave either as a tough guy who never cries, a wiseguy who makes fun of everyone and everything, or a sensitive loner who finds it difficult to relate to extroverted friends. The preadolescent boy is therefore more amenable to sharing ideas and feelings with girls—for whom sharing ideas and feelings tends to be second nature.

Because boys and girls accept one another as individuals at this time of life, they are willing to challenge one another, to be honest about feelings, and to learn to tolerate criticism and disagreement. The child who develops real sensitivity to another's feelings at this age learns to see a relationship not for what he can get out of it but for what he can give. This mutuality is crucial to relationships that will come later in life. When this quality is completely developed, it's called love.

How You Can Encourage
Appropriate Social Skills

You can help your child with opposite-sex relationships by modeling a good male-female bonding yourself. If you and your partner can share ideas, argue and make up, act silly and act serious, lead and follow, your child will be able to see the whole range of possibility in opposite-sex intimacy. It's also a great idea to show that gender-specific behavior doesn't always apply; for example, Dad can cook and clean when Mom's on a business trip, and Mom can shine in a local softball league.

One excellent way for children to hone their skills in this area is for them to join a coed group (a church, 4-H, theatrical, or glee club) or attend a coed overnight camp for a few weeks. These informal associations teach a natural closeness among friends of both sexes. Your child might also want to give a coed party, which you'll plan together. This is another good way for you to help set the tone you want as your child expands her circle of friends and ways of relating to them.

Of course, preparation for coed friendships never guarantees smooth sailing all along the way. You can't rescue your child from embarrassment in early opposite-sex relationships. Let's imagine that Carl was more of a Strong-Willed Child and had decided to take all his part-time job earnings and throw a big surprise party for Cheryl, a Shy Child. If Carl's mother forbade him to do this because she thought Cheryl would be terribly embarrassed and find all the attention painful, she might have provoked a very unpleasant confrontation. Torn between his independent decision to use his own money and give his friend a party and his parents' feelings about inappropriate behavior, Carl might have lashed out at his parents, at Cheryl, or at himself. A ten-to-twelve-year-old's sense of self-worth is enormously fragile, and it's better to let him make his own decisions in this area, even if you feel he may be hurt by the outcome. (You can, however, work on the "Peer-Pressure Puzzles" and "Looking In from the Other Side" exercises to give him more perspective on Cheryl's feelings.)

PEER GROUP/PEER PRESSURE:
"Who cares what they think about me? This is what I want."

Alison, a Team Player who was also a Thinker, found that seventh grade was a lot harder than sixth because of the incredible pressure to be in the "cool" group, where Wendy, a real Boss, called all the shots. Sometimes Wendy would invite Alison to do things with the group; at other times she'd purposely exclude Alison from events. Alison felt torn by the conflict—feeling rotten when excluded, terrific when included.

About two months after the start of the semester, however, Alison started getting friendly with Jo, a Shy Child and a real maverick who wasn't interested in being part of any group. As the two girls got closer, Alison felt her anxiety fading about how important the group was. She didn't *have* to hang around waiting for Wendy to ask her to do things—it just didn't mean that much to her anymore.

On one occasion the kids had a half day off from school, and Alison and Jo decided to spend the free time at the library working on a project. Wendy called Alison the night before to tell her that the gang was getting together for lunch at the local pizza parlor, and could she come? Alison took a deep breath and said she couldn't come the following day, but if the group wanted to change the lunch to Saturday, she'd be there.

She heard Wendy's hesitation on the other end and expected her to say something scathing. Instead Wendy said she'd ask the other girls if they'd be willing to postpone it! When she called back an hour later and said lunch would be on Saturday and that they'd see her there, Alison felt great.

What's Really Going On?

Alison bucked the tide of peer pressure and won. She hadn't *needed* them to want her; she hadn't bent over backward to get the invitation; and she hadn't done anything to hurt Jo. The importance the group had in her life decreased as she realized that she was an autonomous being who could make her own decisions.

The freedom to fluctuate from free agent to group member is vital at this age. Most children—introverts more than extroverts—have difficulty not caring whether or not they're included. Part of the reason for this is that ten-to-twelve-year-olds' social activity is all about the simple act of being together. Preadolescents walk to school together, sit around the library together, talk on the phone, listen to music, go to parties, and hang out at malls or on street corners. Their daily, nightly, and weekend rituals revolve around coming into contact with other kids their age. Family takes a backseat, and friends become paramount influences on opinion, dress, thought, and action.

It would have been too scary for Alison to buck the tide of convention all by herself. She had to feel sure she had an ally—Jo—before she could question Wendy's authority in the group. And she might not have been interested in a friendship with Jo (who had never been hooked on being "in with the in-crowd") had she not been ready to abandon her allegiance to this group. If Alison had been an Adapter, a performer, or a Team Player, she might have found it harder to strike out on her own.

Another important distinction that Alison might make as an independent Thinker is that groups aren't bad, it's just that she might have joined the wrong one. Maybe the idea of belonging was more appealing than the particular niche she was trying to fit herself into. And despite the fact that she has Jo, at some time she may want the comfort of a bigger group of friends.

A parent can help a child decide how she wants to see herself in relation to others. Do spend about fifteen or twenty minutes a day with your older child. Whether you use the structured exercises in this book or just chat, a period of time together gives a continuity to your relationship and assures your child that you're interested in her. You may find that some spot outside the home is more conducive to confiding— you could plan to meet for a soda after school.

You can help your child get at the source of her concerns by underscoring her feelings ("Sounds like you're not sure about camp this summer," or "I can remember when my friend Priscilla was never around when *I* wanted to see her"). Your observations will help your child to see her position more clearly. They will also let her know that "Ms. Popularity" isn't always the most desirable label to have in life. It certainly isn't worth it if you have to spend all your time with people you don't like.

Your Child/Your Role

HAS YOUR CHILD EVER:

- Started dressing, talking, and acting just like the "fast" kids, although her social style is nothing like theirs?
- Turned down an invitation from a close friend because he wasn't "cool"?
- Seemed very depressed because she wasn't asked to join a group for a certain event?
- Stubbornly refused to go along with a seemingly innocuous group decision?

Achieving a balance between peer pressure and personal autonomy is difficult even for adults. This is why your ten-to-twelve-year-old, who is just beginning to figure out where he or she fits in, needs to be able to experiment. If every one of your child's friends is baby-sitting, she may wish to start baby-sitting even if she can't *stand* little kids. If the guys decide to build an electric car for a science fair, your artistic son may suddenly develop a passion for kilowatts. Some days he will stick to the group, some days he will shun the group, and other days he simply won't be able to make up his mind what he wants to do.

How You Can Encourage Appropriate Social Skills

One of the social skills you want to encourage at this time is a sophisticated version of the earlier willingness to participate, tempered by the ability to go against the flow when the situation warrants it. Preteens sometimes bend over backward to get an invitation or just a nod from the group leader, and may actually humiliate themselves in an attempt to fit in.

Remind your child of times when standing up for himself got him where he wanted to be, and give appropriate emotional support. You can let him know it's sometimes hard for you to take an unpopular stand at work or among friends, and that sometimes the benefits of being your own person despite what others expect of you can't be seen until well after the fact. The "Peer-Pressure Puzzles," in Chapter Seven, may also help him to grow more comfortable in his decision making. He'll be able to understand that even if he doesn't make the right choices all the time, at least they're his choices. And next time he can always make different ones.

WARNING SIGNS THAT YOUR CHILD MIGHT NEED HELP

This is a time when children may be on an even keel for months at a time and then suddenly seem to have problems in many areas—in school, at home, among friends. It's perfectly normal for a ten-to-twelve-year-old to go through hard times every once in a while, but if you notice a long spell of depression, anxiety, or acting out, you may want to consult Chapter Nine, "Children Who Can't Reach Out."

In addition ask yourself the following questions about your child. If the answer to several of the items is affirmative *on a regular basis*, your child may need professional help.

- Is your child unable to see anyone else's perspective? Do minor arguments cause a serious breach of friendship?

- Is your child avoiding family entirely?
- Is your child intimidated by any group activity?
- Does your child talk obsessively about the opposite sex or sexual matters? Is she engaging in precocious sexual activity?
- Is your child spending a great deal of time locked in his room? Does he no longer confide in you about anything?
- Does your child seem depressed, lacking appetite, gaining or losing weight?

With the information you now have about your child's preadolescent friendships, you will be able to encourage future personal growth and head off some of the problems of the teen years. As our children become young adults, the social skills they have honed during their early years will afford them exceptional life advantages.

9

CHILDREN WHO CAN'T REACH OUT

Some children have serious social problems that extend beyond the range of what most experts consider acceptable or adaptable. If your child is severely withdrawn or depressed, if he bullies others or acts out his anger in a variety of ways, or if he seems to be engaged in a battle with himself a great deal of the time, it is probably time to consider professional help if you haven't done so already.

Many of these children may be viewed as extremes of the social styles we've delineated in Chapter Two. The Boss who always has to dominate others may become a bully. The Fragile Flower, Thinker, or Shy Child who can't deal with the world may become withdrawn or depressed. The Performer who can never get enough attention may begin to act out. And the child who attempts to reach out to others but who does so without any success may be dyssemic, that is, he may have a learning disability that interferes with his understanding of nonverbal communications.

How can you tell if your child should have a professional

evaluation? It is more difficult to diagnose a problem in a very young child, where social styles and skills are so changeable. But there are certain indications that might lead you to believe that your child needs help, even in the youngest of age groups.

If you examine the "Social Skills and Styles" chart, in Chapter Two, you will note the abilities your child should be developing in the normal course of maturation. He will excel in certain ones, have potential for others, and be weak in some. The child who has severe problems will either have skills missing entirely, be weak in all the skills listed, or have an overabundance of one skill to the exclusion of most of the others (for example, a bully may have leadership ability but cannot temper it with the other necessary social attributes).

DON'T PLACE BLAME

The best thing you can do as a parent is to support your child, no matter what his problems. It's useless to blame him or yourself or society for his emotional dysfunction. There are many reasons why a child may not follow the traditional developmental course.

There are cases when a child with certain strong personality traits is born into a family that just can't handle such differences among members. It's also possible that the family hasn't identified the real difficulty that's making the child act in a certain way. They are paying too much attention to the "trees" (the superficial symptoms) and not enough to the "forest" (the underlying condition). It may be necessary—with professional assistance—to uncover the deeper issues. One other explanation is that the family itself is dysfunctional, and one person's difficulties feed into another's. A final possibility is that the cause is unknown. Just as there are medical mysteries that are beyond the realm of diagnosis, so there are also psychological mysteries. Some children are "wired" in a way that makes them less tractable and more troubled than other children.

But help is available. There is nothing shameful or onerous about therapy. In fact kids who've been lucky enough to get timely counseling often turn out, in later life, to be more self-aware and better equipped to use social skills effectively. If you can look at your child honestly and not despair about a situation that seems out of your control, you can—with the help of a qualified psychologist, psychiatrist, or social worker—get your child back on the right track.

You can get recommendations for excellent professional help through your school guidance department if your child is old enough to attend school, or from a reference from your pediatrician or family physician. All therapists should be state-licensed. You should have periodic consultations with the professional who is helping your child in order to follow up on the prognosis and treatment and so that you can work with your child at home along the lines the therapist suggests.

We are going to discuss five frequently observed types of social maladaptation. The first two typically affect an introverted child; the last three affect an extroverted child. There are of course different permutations of these five, but the signs and symptoms in the following areas are common to many children with problems:

- The withdrawn child
- The depressed child
- The bully
- The acting-out child
- The inappropriate socializer, who can't make her behavior meet others' expectations

THE WITHDRAWN CHILD

Richard was a sensitive, physically frail only child, a Thinker and Fragile Flower. Although he would play with other kids, he clearly enjoyed his own company better. He learned to read at the age of four, and by the time he was five, he spent most of his time after school at his computer. His mother, an administrator in the local school system, was a warm and compassionate woman with a great sense of humor. His father, a university professor who prided himself on his excellent library, encouraged Richard's academic achievements and always made time to be with his son.

Richard was six when his father died of a heart attack. His mother, who had been more of a Firm Guider than his father, was initially depressed, but because of her concern about Richard's sensitivity, she was able to put her grief aside to be a strong support for her son. She reminded him of the good times the three of them had shared and made up special events for the two of them to enjoy. She did everything she could to try to boost his spirits, but it was like talking into a vacuum. Richard just didn't respond—he couldn't laugh or cry with her.

Richard withdrew from life, saying he felt too tired for most activities. He hated any mention of his father's death. He was sick a lot and avoided school as much as he could. The few friends he did have got tired of being rebuffed when they tried to play with him. Consequently by age seven Richard had few opportunities to hone his social skills.

His mother simply couldn't stand by and watch her son retreat from life. She made an appointment for him with the guidance counselor at school, and on the counselor's recommendation she got him into therapy. Slowly Richard began to open up. After about a year the wall he'd built around himself began to crumble. Although books were still his friends, the links he forged to reach his father, he was now less withdrawn and began to be interested in other children.

Recognizing the Withdrawn Child

If your child exhibits several of the following symptoms, he may be *withdrawn:*

- He always refuses playdates or group activities
- She has a single preoccupation—her books, her music, her computer, her artwork—and they are too important to allow time for anything or anyone else
- She loves to daydream—it's often hard to distract her from her private world
- She shows little interest in others' problems
- He is enthusiastic only about solitary activities

Why would your child become withdrawn? Often the reason is that he has found the pain of attachment too great, just as Richard did. If you invest a lot of love and care in another person—a parent or a friend—and that person goes away or rebuffs you, it may be too much to take. You protect yourself by not getting involved with others so that you can't be hurt by them.

The child who shuns other people may become a loner with a rich, detailed fantasy life. He may also do a lot of "self-parenting," giving himself limitations and restrictions as well as rewards and support. Actually the fact that he takes care of himself is good, adaptive behavior, and it does keep him functioning, but it also insulates him from friends and relatives. His relationships with others may seem shallow and underdeveloped. Instead of enjoying the dialogue most of us have daily with our friends and acquaintances, he sets up his life as an interior monologue.

The withdrawn child says he likes it this way, but underneath he may be terribly lonely. He may feel unworthy of friendship and terrified of the prospect of being rejected by a friend.

There is a big difference between a lonely child and one who simply enjoys being alone sometimes—which is a positive response to life. For example, the child who opts for an afternoon by himself with a good book and some CDs is having a good time. Later he'll have a good time by calling a friend or going to a Cub Scout meeting. He is flexible in his social choices.

Many withdrawn children are reacting to some aspect of family life that they find upsetting. They take this issue to an extreme in their fantasy life and magnify it to such a degree that it dominates their actions and reactions. A sensitive parent may be able to pick up on this before her child gets too far off course. If you can identify the culprit event or emotion, you may be able to correct your child's distorted point of view. Sometimes, however, in a situation such as Richard's, even the most aware parent is not able to break through the barricade that the child has set up.

If you sense that you cannot help your child because your own problems seem overwhelming, if you are having trouble connecting to your partner or to others, or if you find yourself distracted and unable to "be there" for your child, you should seek help yourself. A therapist will help you to reorient yourself to parenting, and this in turn will tend to make you feel more functional in other aspects of your life. Of course if there are serious family problems such as abuse or alcoholism, they must be handled professionally as well.

In addition to counseling help you can do a lot of good for your child's self-esteem by talking about your family situation honestly and compassionately. Many children feel ashamed of themselves if their parent has a problem. They need help understanding that they aren't responsible for the problem and that they cannot cure their parent. Pay attention to your child's nonverbal messages. Listen to him when he asks for attention—however indirectly. And acknowledge his feelings when he is able to express them. Take every opportunity to encourage his talents and skills so that he can feel good about himself again.

Understanding the Very Young Withdrawn Child

The very young withdrawn child, from eighteen months to five years, will have trouble playing in a group. When a nursery school teacher calls everyone together for Simon Says or a clapping game, this child will usually sit passively to one side. She may not even focus her eyes on the activity in the room. Her reaction to her friends' trouble or pain may be minimal to nonexistent: If she saw another child fall and cut her arm in the playground, she might not comfort her or go to summon a teacher.

The reason for this lack of emotional response is usually because it's hard to feel empathy when you are so tightly drawn into your own world. The withdrawn child is often protected from the stress and turmoil around her because she doesn't allow it to penetrate emotionally.

The younger withdrawn child will need a professional evaluation so that her problem can be diagnosed. In addition you as parent can do a lot to help her through difficult times. Gently encourage her to play with others and help her with transitions from one activity to the next by telling her in advance about one event ending and another beginning. For example, if you're baking cookies and a friend is coming over, you could have your child set aside a plate of cookies for her friend. After discussing your plan with your child so that she feels included, you might make a one-on-one playdate every week or so with another child who is very social—a Team Player or Adapter—and supervise their play to make sure the children are interacting. Structured games where each child has to contribute an idea or a type of activity are good spurs to getting the withdrawn child involved.

You will also need to do some self-evaluating. Is the atmosphere in your home angry or upsetting? Do you spend enough time with your child each day? How do you behave with your friends? If you can model being openly friendly with others, it will help your child to move ahead in her own way of relating.

Be sure to talk to your child a lot. A withdrawn child tends to be overly quiet. If you can model more outgoing behavior, it may stimulate her to be more expansive. You can also articulate her thoughts and feelings for her temporarily while she's learning to relate more openly to others. For example, you might comment on how big and brave she looked on the swing in the playground and ask if it made her feel like she was flying when she went up so high. By starting her off with a description of an incident, you may encourage her to add ideas of her own.

Understanding the Older Withdrawn Child

An older withdrawn child, from five to twelve years of age, who is developmentally ready for life but can't take part it in, needs more intensive care. She will already have certain rituals that are hard to break—coming directly home from school and locking her door, refusing to talk with friends on the phone, disappearing from family occasions to read in her room. She may make it difficult or impossible for others to include her in group activities. For example, if she is required to participate in a school play, she may vanish into the bathroom during rehearsals or conveniently get sick on the night of the performance.

You cannot simply arrange activities for the older with-drawn child as you can for the younger. What can you do in addition to therapy? Before tackling the outside social world, begin with your family situation. The more comfortable you can make it at home, the better. Take twenty minutes each day when you have no other distractions to sit and talk or do some activity with your child. This will reduce his loneliness and give him a reason to believe in the power of relatedness. It doesn't matter what you do or how awkward you may feel—just devote the time to being together. As he grows more comfortable with you, he may start to give you clues as to what might be wrong and what he needs from you.

Next take a look at your attitude toward your child and that of your partner. Ask yourself honestly if there is any conflict you're not dealing with. Do you belittle your child's abilities? Do you yell at him a lot for minor infractions? The mildest criticism that would roll off the back of a Team Player or Performer can really cripple a sensitive child.

You should also consider your own social patterns. Are you a loner, or do you see friends on a very irregular basis? By getting yourself more socially active, you can provide a model for your child. Have you isolated yourself from friends and family? If so, make a conscious effort to reconnect with others. Invite people in for casual meals or a cup of coffee; have a few family dinner parties or backyard barbecues. In-volve your child by planning the event with him, asking him to help with the cooking or setting the table or answering the door. He could also photograph the occasion for you. Don't pester him into having conversations—let him just be there physically, and soon he may wish to be there emotionally.

THE DEPRESSED CHILD

Marilyn was a Thinker and Strong-Willed Child, the second oldest of four children. Her mother was often busy with her baby sister, who had chronic allergies. Her father, who managed a trucking business, was a Tough Guy in his parenting style, and he set down a lot of rules and regulations for the children to follow.

Marilyn always seemed angry after playing with other children. Even at the age of five she criticized all the kids in her class. They were too bossy, or too messy to play with. She said that some of the girls who were more physically agile than she made her feel dumb and clumsy when they were on the playground together. Marilyn seemed to start each morning unhappy with the prospect of what was to come ("I just know this is going to be a terrible day") no matter what was in the offing.

Unlike the withdrawn child, who keeps her unhappiness to herself, many depressed children let everyone know how miserable they are. Marilyn was surly and difficult in her second-grade class project group, insisting that the clay animal she was making wasn't good enough to bake in the kiln. The other children and the teacher disagreed, but after Marilyn's ceramic dog came out of the oven, Marilyn pointed out that his ears weren't straight. She was so angry, she smashed the dog. When she came home and complained to her mother, she blamed herself. "I never do anything right," she said hopelessly.

Marilyn, like other depressed children, feels abandoned and misunderstood. If only her parents could spend more time with her. If only the other kids and the teacher had recognized that she had to work harder on her dog—but they just didn't care about her. Her sense of loss goes deep and may have to do with her mother's intense involvement with her sister or with her father's high expectations for perfect behavior. Marilyn's depression is her way of crying out for help.

Recognizing the Depressed Child

If your child is exhibiting several of the following symptoms, she may be *depressed:*

- He is angry all the time and takes it out on himself
- She feels ugly and hates her body
- She regularly compares herself unfavorably to others
- He has little interest in his schoolwork or any other activity
- She has no appetite, or eats erratically
- More rarely, he is overactive (this might be a defense against his depression)

Understanding the Very Young Depressed Child

The young depressed child may appear to be a Naysayer most of the time. It's hard for him to get along with friends because he feels that nothing is any good, including the people he associates with. Although he more typically takes out his anger and anxiety on himself, he may also be irritated around other children and not want to spend any time with them.

Depression in a young child is very often a symptom of feeling stranded—left alone by parents or by the world in general. A thoughtful, self-reflective five-year-old whose parents both work and who has a succession of baby-sitters may feel that nobody wants him or cares about him.

An excellent method of dealing with a young depressed child is to structure time specifically around his needs. This might mean a nightly bedtime story (you read to him and he reads to you) or allowing him to help plan a special outing or event each weekend. Make sure that whatever time period and activity you select is *all* for him and that there are no disruptions.

Uninterrupted time may be a problem if you have several children. This may mean recruiting a grandparent or getting more baby-sitting help so that more of your time can be allocated to this child, at least until he's over some of his biggest emotional hurdles.

If he is having academic or social problems at school, be sure you discuss this with his teachers, the guidance counselor, and the principal in order to develop a plan together that will help him.

Understanding the Older Depressed Child

The older depressed child is more typically female than male. According to a 1990 study by psychologists Betty Merten and Peter Lewinsohn, at the Oregon Research Institute in Portland, girls are twice as likely as boys to feel depressed. This was further substantiated by a study at Columbia University by psychiatrist Dr. Agnes Whitaker, who states that "girls have higher rates of both mild and major depression than do boys."

Girls seems to feel a lot of stress, particularly in the eight-to-twelve-year-old age groups, about body image and social acceptability. They are often obsessed by their appearance and the desire for others to find them attractive. Boys of this age are allowed to feel good about themselves through participation in sports (although they may become anxious about how well they measure up on a team). Though girls may have sports as an outlet, too, their excellence in athletics doesn't always make up for feelings of low self-esteem.

Although depression is more prevalent in girls this age, they may be better equipped than boys to deal with their problems because they tend to be more verbally expressive about their feelings. This means that two depressed girls can be great foils for each other, helping each other to look at problems more objectively. Boys' talks together may be less emotionally oriented than girls', but they are still usually capable of sharing deep feelings with one another about being lonely or different in some way.

Peer discussion seems to be an excellent method of handling depression in older children. Getting kids to talk together and reevaluate their perceived failures—be they personal, social, or academic—can be helpful in banishing self-defeating thoughts. Kids can share highly sensitive subjects and get an objective hearing on them from friends without fear of censure or ridicule. Discussion groups can be found in school settings, in churches and synagogues, and in other youth organizations. Since this technique works so well, you should seriously consider getting your depressed child involved in a discussion group.

Talking things out is important as a family, too, since it allows the depressed child to feel that you really care about him. You can also help your child attack depression by scheduling a purely relaxing activity that you enjoy doing together, such as skating, biking, a puzzle, or a crafts project.

It's common for the older depressed child to lose interest in school and drop out of extracurricular activities. After talking with her teachers and guidance counselor, you might also consider hiring a home tutor. If she starts getting better grades or joins some clubs or school projects, her mood will improve and she may have more control over her depressed periods.

It's important to think about underlying causes of your child's depression that aren't so readily apparent. Many children who become aware that they may be homosexual or who are having confusion about their sexual orientation will become depressed because they feel isolated in their difference. It's easy to understand why a child who is afraid to confess to his parents that he thinks he may be gay would feel abandoned. It's vital that you show your child you approve of *him* regardless of your feelings about his sexual orientation. It's advisable to work as a family with a therapist so that you can make sense of this issue together.

THE BULLY

Jack was a large child, weighing over eleven pounds at birth. He walked early, but didn't start using words effectively until he was nearly two. Jack was a Boss and a Strong-Willed Child, and it was difficult for his mother, a timid woman who had always shied away from confrontation, to control him during a temper tantrum.

Jack couldn't stand it when another child took a toy and would physically shove the child, throw the toy at him, or try to dominate him in some way. He was enrolled in a nursery school, but the teachers found him so disruptive that his parents were asked to take him out of school. He would typically pull a chair out from under the child next to him if he wanted to sit in it and would often hit that child once he was on the floor.

Jack's mother didn't know how to handle him. She had never felt comfortable with the role of mother, and she had little confidence in her parenting skills. Jack's father, a Tough Guy in his parenting style, had no hesitation about spanking his son for misbehaving, and he urged his wife to do the same when he wasn't around.

When Jack was only ten, he had his first encounter with the law one winter after pushing another child off a small bridge into icy water. Jack's parents' next-door neighbor accused him of poisoning her dog in the Letters to the Editor column of the town newspaper. After this incident (which was never proven), Jack made it a point to threaten and humiliate the neighbor whenever he could. Throughout his elementary and junior-high years he spent more time in the principal's and guidance counselor's offices than he did in the classroom.

Recognizing the Bully

If your child exhibits several of the following symptoms, he may be a *bully:*

- He thinks life is "unfair" and that people are "out to get" him
- She always reacts physically to a stressful confrontation with a friend
- She is unfazed by name-calling or belittling—things just "roll off" her
- He is fascinated by war heroes, dictators, criminals
- He doesn't "feel" anything when he causes someone else pain and seems happy only when he is dominating others

Bullies have often been persuaded from their earliest days that they are "worthless," "stupid," "chicken," or "bad." For this reason they try to reverse their feeling of low self-esteem by making others feel the way they've been made to feel.

Bullies are typically children who are mismatched with a very ineffectual or inconsistent parent and who may also be engaged in a power struggle with a domineering parent. Bullies almost always have been bullied themselves. A child who has been beaten up by his father for not getting out of bed on time will often beat up a smaller child on his way to school. He can't get back at his overwhelmingly powerful father, but he can reverse the power position with a smaller target—the kid down the block or even (as he develops and becomes physically larger) his siblings or his mother.

Deep down, of course, bullies feel powerless. They feel small and insignificant in comparison to their abusive parent, and the only way they can start to feel effective again is to exert power in any way possible. They are unable to feel empathy and consideration for themselves or for others—even when abused, they usually claim they "don't care" or it "didn't hurt." Bullying can be a way of dealing with depression. By "not feeling" and abusing others, bullies try to suppress their own pain and sadness.

Bullies thrive on intimidation and control. The opponent who stands up for himself or says that he won't fight isn't worth tormenting, so the bully generally walks away from this inappropriate target, deeming him "dumb." This is an excellent thing to remember if you are currently being terrorized by your child or if your child is the target of a bully.

Bullies and the Family Power Structure

If you have seen your child bullying others or if he bullies you, you are going to have to do some serious thinking about your family structure and power plays. Before you can help your child, you must figure out—on your own or with the help of a therapist—why your child acts as he does. Ask yourself the following questions:

• Is your child imitating someone else in the family—a spouse, a grandparent, an uncle?

• Why does he feel so powerless that he must intimidate others in order to feel strong?

• How does your family share power? Is one person always responsible for making decisions?

• Does your child have a fair say in family matters? Or does no one ever pay attention to his requests?

Understanding the Very Young Bully

Certain children, particularly Strong-Willed/Naysayers, may be very difficult to handle for parents whose natural inclination is to let things go. A mother who is either Inconsistent or a Worrier in her parenting style doesn't know how to react properly to the infant who hurls an empty bottle at her, nor to the toddler who pummels another child to get a toy. The combination of very strong child and very weak parent may produce a bully. (This syndrome is more common among boys, but there are girl bullies as well.) The toddler bully is unable to participate in group activities or to follow rules because he must be in charge all the time. He will get his way or his toy in any manner possible, without consideration for anyone else's physical space or emotional needs.

If you can recognize the conflict of power between your child and another family member, you are halfway toward a solution. Your job is to promote a more positive relationship between the young bully and the adult who intimidates your child at home. This will, of course, require that adult to be truly willing to change his own behavior.

Naturally you will want to model appropriate behavior for your child, redirect bullying tendencies toward constructive play, and be supportive when he is able to moderate his actions. Frequently, an organized program of behavior modification can really make inroads into this problem. For example, let's take a three-year-old who hits other children in order to get toys and whose mother is always critical or physically punitive toward the child. In order to change the way these two relate to each other, you might set up a reward system. Each time the child is able to deal with her anger or frustration with words instead of fists, she is given a gold star on a chart. Once she has earned five stars, she gets a soda or ice-cream cone with her mother. During their time together the mother will emphasize how pleased she is with her daughter's progress. Naturally the technique will work on both mother and daughter, because they are getting positive reinforcement out of their time together rather than their usual negative reinforcement.

Understanding the Older Bully

An older, bigger bully is a more difficult challenge because he has had more time to perfect the power-play situation and his emotional responses are much more ingrained at this age. A bully can be physically, mentally, or emotionally cruel, usually to a smaller, weaker child.

Behavior-modification programs, such as the one outlined above, can work for both child and parent. If you have a ten-year-old bully who has fallen behind in his schoolwork, he might be rewarded for five consecutive nights of completing his homework by having an outing with his father. His father might assist with his homework or look it over when it has finished, stressing that he's pleased with his son's progress and looking forward to their excursion together. The more positive the interaction between them, the better. A parent-child bond can help break the bully's feelings of low self-esteem that had caused him to act like a bully in the first place.

Bullies who have already been in trouble with the law will be monitored by a child-guidance specialist or social worker assigned by the police. You must work closely with this outside professional. Many therapists recommend community-service programs, which can be fruitful and enriching for everyone involved. Learning that he has the power to put things back together again will teach a bully more than any punishment.

Intensive therapy with the right counselor—one who is firm but fair—is essential for the older bully. He must feel that he has someone who really listens to him and understands. A male therapist who balances strength and compassion can reinforce the notion of a powerful father figure who is also a good guy.

THE ACTING-OUT CHILD

Maryanne was extremely Strong-Willed, a Performer who needed to be in the limelight. Many neighbors referred to her as the wild child. She had no interest in following rules.

Maryanne rode off on her bike one day when she was six and was missing for two hours before she was found by the police about three miles from home. At eleven she was caught shoplifting at the local five-and-dime; and at twelve she was known in school as a fast girl because she dressed in provocative clothing and allowed boys to "feel her up."

Maryanne's parents were divorced when she was five, and she lived with her mother and her older sister. Maryanne's father had moved out of state with his new wife, and the girls saw him infrequently. Although her mother tried to parent, she was depressed and inadequate and tended to favor her older daughter, who behaved well and took care of her mother. Maryanne always complained about her "perfect sister" and claimed that her parents loved Josephine more.

In high school Maryanne's moods began to fluctuate wildly. Sometimes she seemed exuberant about life; at other times she was terribly depressed. She stole from the supermarket and convenience store on several occasions.

Until about the age of eight Maryanne had several friends who were Followers, but as she got older and her acting-out behavior became more serious, they were forbidden by their parents to spend time with her. Her companions tended to be older and male.

In this instance, counseling was urgently needed for the entire family.

Recognizing the Acting-Out Child

If your child exhibits several of the following symptoms, he may be acting out:

- He is aggressive and picks fights for no reason
- She is intractable—will run away or fight back instead of accepting discipline
- He is destructive to property
- She may indulge in precocious sexual behavior
- He may steal or shoplift
- She may spend most of her time with other children who are branded as "different" or "problem kids"

Understanding the Very Young Acting-Out Child

The child who acts out may be covering up depression. His brash behavior may be a way of throwing off his feelings of worthlessness.

It is enormously important that you set limits for the younger child. Your attitude as parent must be firm but sympathetic, with stress on the former. Since this child is always pushing against the limits, it's important for him to know where he's supposed to be and when. This type of child should have a schedule—a regular bedtime, mealtime, and playtime.

His aggressive attitude toward other kids may make it difficult for him to attract and sustain friendships. Here again you can help by inviting playmates to your home and monitoring any wild behavior. If your child gets into a confrontation in a day-care setting or at preschool, be sure you and the teacher are in accord as to how to handle it. Any disputes should be resolved verbally rather than physically. Never compare your child to anyone else, and extend praise whenever you can—particularly when he's handled a social situation well.

Modeling balanced, reasonable behavior in your own marriage and friendships and in your behavior toward your child is enormously important. As with the bully, it's important for you to spend private time with your child to try to fathom what might be making her so unhappy. The "bad" behavior is always a way of attracting attention; if you can give her attention for appropriate or neutral behavior, she may begin to find that acting out is less appealing.

Therapists often use role-playing to get at the underlying causes for acting out in a young child. A doll's house or puppet theater will give your child the ability to move people and situations around and in so doing explain her frustrations and anger to the therapist.

Understanding the Older Acting-Out Child

An older child who acts out needs firmness combined with a lot of love and attention. A child who runs off, destroys property, or indulges in sexual escapades is begging for supportive structure and appropriate discipline.

It will be vital for you to know where she is at all times. You and she should fill out a schedule so that certain times are reserved each day for homework, household chores, activities, and friends.

You should also set aside family time each day. This child is crying out for nurturing and needs your attention. Let her plan a menu one night a week and set aside that time to prepare and share a family meal. You can also structure a nightly relaxation period where you can talk, play music, and just spend time together.

Although you can't always be well acquainted with every one of your child's friends, it's important that she spend the majority of her time with people her own age whom you trust. As you do more talking together as a family, she may want to confide in you more about her feelings and frustrations. The acting-out child usually isn't interested in pleasing a parent the way the withdrawn or depressed child might be. But this is a two-way street. You need to work on your relationship with her and show her that you care so that she will be more motivated to take your opinions into account when choosing her friends.

If you aren't able to work effectively with your child, you will undoubtedly want to discuss more radical changes with a therapist, particularly if you find that you are overly punitive when she breaks the rules and gets into trouble. In some instances, your therapist may wish to counsel you to structure a temporary living arrangement for your child with a relative or friend who is less emotionally involved. It's essential for you and the therapist to explain this situation to your child in a positive way. You should never imply that she is being abandoned or "sent away" because she was "bad," but rather that everyone involved needs a fresh perspective on the family's problems. Even if you're not living under the same roof, family therapy should continue and can help you to understand why your child is so unhappy and why she does the hurtful things she does.

THE INAPPROPRIATE SOCIALIZER

Todd never reacted to situations the way any other child might react. His mother never knew exactly what to expect from him, even when he was a baby. He was certainly Adaptable, yet he was very Strong-Willed, sometimes to an infuriating degree. He was a Performer, or actually a cutup—the class clown—as soon as he started nursery school.

Todd would do embarrassing things in public—pick his

nose or masturbate in public—and any number of talks from his parents about how these were private activities never seemed to sink in. In kindergarten, when one little girl described how sad she felt because her dog had died, Todd immediately got up and mimed being the dog getting shot in the head and rolling over with his legs sticking up in the air. When the little girl began crying, Todd started barking and laughing hysterically.

On a more subtle level Todd didn't "click" with anyone else. He'd talk when they were talking, or walk away in the middle of a conversation. It wasn't that he had no consideration for others; rather it was as if he couldn't quite make the distinction between himself and others. His most severe lack was in the area of nonverbal communication. He just didn't pick up hints from those around him that what he was doing was inappropriate or out of sync. The boundaries of his world were loose and unstructured.

Recognizing the Inappropriate Socializer

Psychologists Stephen Nowicki, Jr., and Marshall P. Duke, from Emory University in Atlanta, have defined the learning disorder "dyssemia" as the inability to understand, or the tendency to miss, social signals given by others. The syndrome was coined from two Greek words—*dys*, which means "difficulty," and *semes*, which means "signals." This learning disability affected nearly 10 percent of children tested for this disorder in the 1990 Emory study of several thousand children. If your child exhibits several of the following symptoms, he may have dyssemia:

- He stands too close when he talks to someone, invading the other person's space
- He picks his nose, masturbates, or does other inappropriate behavior in public

- Her emotions aren't in sync with anyone else's—she may laugh when something sad happens
- He has facial or verbal tics
- She abruptly switches topics in mid-sentence
- She stares rudely at people or says something personal about them so that they can clearly hear, not realizing that it may hurt their feelings

Only recently has this disorder had a name; previously kids who just didn't "get it" socially were shunned and maligned by peers and adults alike. Their body language, facial expressions, posture, tone of voice, even their manner of dressing were different. They were always the last ones picked for teams and the ones who got ridiculed to their faces. Parents and teachers may not be aware of what is going on until the dyssemic child is already quite advanced in the syndrome. The unfortunate part of this is that usually by the time the parents or teacher have identified the problem, the child has already lost a considerable amount of self-esteem and feels awkward and out of place in any social context.

Understanding the Inappropriate Socializer

Many parents who suspect that their child might be emotionally disturbed may be relieved to discover that the problem is actually dyssemia, a very treatable learning disability. By using the informal assessment guide offered by Drs. Nowicki and Duke in their book (see the Bibliography at the end of this book), you and the caregiver or teacher most familiar with your child will probably be able to handle this relearning technique without professional assistance.

Ninety out of one hundred dyssemic children are missing some nonverbal processing skills that can be taught to them relatively easily in a home or school setting. The other 10 percent may need professional therapy and will be helped by a remediation program managed by learning-disability therapists familiar with the Emory University method.

But for most children with dyssemia there are specific guidelines for discriminating different nonverbal communication skills that you and your child's caregiver or teacher can use. The Emory University program is applicable to children of all ages—the methods are adaptable to every developmental stage. Play therapy is used for the very young dyssemic child, and verbal puzzles and situations are used for the older child.

The six areas covered in the Emory program are timing skills, touching and distance skills, gestures and postures skills, facial-expressions skills, sound-quality skills, and dress and hygiene skills. Your child may have trouble in one or several or even all of these areas.

In order to help a dyssemic child make sense of other people's body language and facial expressions, for example, you can use your Social Skills Playkit photos (see Chapter Two). First, you can just ask your child to differentiate between two different faces. Second, you can explore the idea of emotion—which face is happy and which is sad. Third, you'll ask your child to put those expressions on his own face. Finally, you'll have him make up situations where he must use the different emotions appropriately. ("My cat got sick, so I feel sad, and this is how my face shows it." "I just got an ice-cream cone, and I feel happy, and this is how my face shows it.")

You can also use television programs as teaching tools. For example, you and your child watch a program with the sound turned off, then play a guessing game as to what people are doing and saying based on the way they stand, sit, and move.

A tape recorder is a useful tool to help a dyssemic child hear how he sounds when he speaks. You can prerecord a few sentences and play them for your child; then you can have him repeat them into the tape recorder. The next step is for you to change the intonation, volume, and emphasis of the sentences and ask your child to try to mimic the changes. An older child can make up the text of what he's saying himself and can then alter the meaning and tone in increasingly subtle ways. For example, he could practice saying something as though he were happy and then see how he might use the same words but change the inflection to show he was angry.

The younger child can be reminded that it's important to keep clean and neat; the older child who is naturally more autonomous in his dress and hygiene habits may need some skills practice by watching people on TV, on the street, or in the mall. Just being with your child in public will afford you numerous opportunities to discuss the varieties and appropriateness of appearance.

The helpful exercises will simply give you some structure as you point out examples of rule-of-thumb social behavior. You'll work on basic social communications, such as greeting someone in the supermarket or meeting another child in the playground. Always you'll want to reinforce nonverbal skills, such as how close to stand to others, how loudly to speak, how to interpret nonverbal cues, and how to moderate behavior so that it coincides with others' expectations.

TO GREATER SOCIAL INTELLIGENCE FOR ALL

We are born with an innate desire and ability to mix and mingle with others. The warming touch of a pal's hand, the compassion in a good friend's eyes, the comaraderie of a cohesive group, can carry us through the worst of times.

Our children need to have practice in fighting and making up, in developing close relationships that overcome differences and boundaries, and in daily, routine respect for others and for their opinions.

A child who can't reach out now isn't doomed. There are many avenues of help available—through schools, therapists, specialized psychological centers—but mostly through you the parent. If you reach out and provide loving support, your child cannot help but feel it. Growing as a parent means sometimes looking at your son or daughter in a way that is painful for you to see. But the rewards that both of you will reap in the end may astound you.

Child or adult, we can learn more about ourselves as we open ourselves up to friends. By nurturing others we learn to care more about the world outside our own personal microcosm. In touching another we join hands in the great dance of humanity. The world is made up of Followers, Adapters, Performers, Thinkers, Bosses, Fragile Flowers, Strong-Willed, and Shy people. Together we are the human family, emotionally sounder and finer than we could ever be alone.

EPILOGUE: A STORY OF A TRUE FRIENDSHIP

Grace, a Performer and Thinker, met Margie, a Thinker and Team Player, when they were both six. They sat across the room from each other in Sunday school, but always gravitated toward each other during break and after school.

When the girls were eight, Grace's parents moved, so the girls were now in the same public-school district. They found, to their surprise and delight, that they were in the same third-grade class.

Their relationship grew closer daily. They were true "chums"—they had a relationship that meshed empathy and give-and-take leadership skills. They could agree to disagree, even at the age of eight. Grace and Margie consolidated their special feelings toward each other with secret jokes and similar clothing. Their other friends laughingly called them Marge-Grace, joining them by name. The girls did their homework at the library together after school, walked to Margie's bus stop together, and made it a point to arrange at least one meal or playdate per weekend. They had lots of sleep-overs throughout the year. Though their parents never became socially friendly, the girls were bonded.

When Grace was ten, her parents told her that they were divorcing. She fled to her room and called Margie, who stayed on the phone with her for an hour, reluctant to hang up because her friend was crying so hard. Early the next morning Margie showed up at Grace's house—even though it was a six-block detour and it was bitterly cold out—to walk her best friend to school. She swore she wouldn't leave her alone until she felt better and even offered to let Grace come and live with her and her family for a while, at least until her parents were settled.

As the divorce moved toward finality, Grace replaced her acute anxiety about her parents with fear that she'd have to move away from Margie. That separation seemed almost worse to her than her parents'. But thankfully her mother got the house in the settlement, and Grace and Margie stayed in the same class. Over the next year Margie was fiercely protective of her friend, defending her if she ever heard anyone talking behind her back.

The intensity of their friendship leveled out a little when the girls entered high school. There were so many new clubs and extracurricular activities to join! Grace was in all the school plays; Margie was busy with the student government. Although their interests had diverged slightly, their friendship remained solid. They were able to get together and compare notes and feelings about the different activities they now participated in.

When Grace started dating Adam, Margie acted as a sounding board. Margie, who didn't have a boyfriend, was only slightly jealous of the romance, because she saw how much her friend still needed her.

The girls graduated first and third in their senior high school class, and both attended college in the East, about an hour's train ride away from each other. Throughout freshman year they still faithfully wedged in some weekend time together. Both girls had their first sexual experiences that year, and they relied on each other to get over the hurts and share the joys. Margie was sure she was in love; Grace tried to be objective and gave her friend a little more perspective on her boyfriend.

Sophomore year the friends didn't see each other much at all. They were both incredibly busy, and the interests of their respective lives made them concentrate much more on being with other people than with each other. And when Margie went to France on her junior year abroad, the girls had to handle their first separation.

Margie formed other friendships that year, but she knew herself well enough to say that none of them had the same depth or closeness as her bond with Grace. And when she got the long-distance phone call in the middle of the night that her father had dropped dead of a heart attack, Grace was the first person she called.

Margie flew back home the next day, and Grace met her at the airport. She was a buffer for her friend throughout the difficult days ahead, even helping with the postfuneral gathering. She held Margie together, listened a lot, fielded phone calls for the family, and made sure Margie remembered to write thank-yous for the condolence cards she received.

The girls both got jobs in different states after college. Grace was an assistant at a magazine in Philadelphia; Margie went to work for a social services agency in Chicago and started on her doctorate in psychology. They talked on the phone infrequently and got together perhaps twice a year. Margie was really involved with a man she knew she would marry, and Grace found that although she wasn't that crazy about Simon, she had to admit he was good for Margie.

Grace was the maid of honor at their wedding. She had some pangs about losing part of her specialness in Margie's life, but she was mature enough to absorb the sadness and look forward to what their relationship might be like in the future.

Grace visited Margie and Simon periodically, and Simon pointed out that whenever the friends had spent about half an hour together, their voice patterns and laughs were absolutely identical. "It's like my wife changes into someone else when she's with you," he said, shaking his head.

But on one visit the three of them got into a discussion about kids. Margie had been traveling a lot on business, and Simon was a filmmaker who was still struggling for recognition. The couple was not exactly settled, according to Grace. She first suggested that they consider waiting to have children. But when both Margie and Simon ganged up on her and told her she had no way of knowing what the right time was for them, Grace lost perspective. She bluntly stated that she didn't think Margie would make a good mother.

Margie was shocked and hurt, and she accused Grace of being jealous because she wasn't in love and married like Margie. The argument escalated. Grace couldn't face Margie the next morning. She drove off before her friend was awake, leaving a note saying that she had some stuff to work out.

It took about a year to settle the dispute. There were apologies and retractions and excuses and all kinds of explanations for the unpleasantness. Grace was finally able to reflect on what had happened and realized that although her point about waiting to have kids had been well taken, she had lashed out at her friend because of some anger at her own unsettled life situation. But things weren't fully resolved until five years later, when Margie gave birth to Zoe.

Without any mention of the ugly argument Grace came to stay for a week and help out. She did dishes, she went grocery shopping, she sat up with Simon after Margie had zonked out with the baby. She felt needed and useful, but the unmentionable argument ate at her. Until Margie brought it up.

Grace admitted that she'd been wrong in her estimation of Margie as a potential mother and that even if she'd been right, that was the sort of hunch you keep to yourself. Saying such a hurtful thing was really awful and detrimental to their friendship.

Margie pointed out that there was more to it. She thought that Grace still hadn't resolved her own dilemma about marriage and children. The baby brought her life into sharp contrast with that of her best friend. Margie was working, too, but she was doing all those "woman" things—and Grace had only her career. She enjoyed herself, she had men friends and had had lovers, but she wasn't a wife or a mother. Margie had leaped ahead of her, and she felt anxious about when—or if—she'd catch up. Margie, miraculously, understood Grace's longings even better than Grace herself did.

Of course Grace did "catch up" eventually. Margie and Simon stood up with Grace when she married Rob two years later. By a very strange coincidence both husbands of the two best friends had the identical birth date, although they were eight years apart in age. "Karma," Grace giggled. "The only reason we married them," Margie stated flatly. And when a daughter was born to Grace and Rob three years later, the circle was completed.

At forty-six these two women are still best friends. One lives in New Jersey, the other in Massachusetts. They see each other infrequently, but they talk on the phone. And both husbands agree that it seems to calm each woman just to hear the other's voice. They talk in shorthand, knowing without having to say much at all what the other is going through. They still share secrets (some of which are even secret from their husbands), and they are still able to fight and make up, to lead and to follow, to sit silent and listen as the other reveals a confidence or tells a joke.

Their intimacy has spilled over into their relationships with their families and their other friends and into their work lives, giving them the skills to deal effectively with all kinds of people. And their dearest hope is that their daughters will find someone just as important as they did to be a lifelong companion of mind and spirit. Just like Grace and Margie.

Friends.

RECOMMENDED READING

BOOKS FOR PARENTS

Stephen R. Asher and John D. Coie. *Peer Rejection in Childhood.* Cambridge, Mass: Cambridge University Press, 1992.

Lawrence Balter. *Dr. Balter's Child Sense.* New York: Poseidon Press 1985.

————. *Who's in Control? Dr. Balter's Guide to Discipline Without Combat.* New York: Poseidon Press, 1989.

Bruno Bettelheim. *The Uses of Enchantment.* New York: Vintage Books, 1976.

T. Berry Brazelton. *Toddlers and Parents.* New York: Dell Publishing Co., 1989.

Stella Chess, M.D., and Alexander Thomas, M.D. *Know Your Child.* New York: Basic Books, 1987.

William Damon. *The Moral Child: Nurturing Children's Natural Moral Growth.* New York: The Free Press, 1988.

Nancy Eisenberg. *The Caring Child.* Cambridge, Mass.: Harvard University Press, 1992.

Erik Erikson. *Childhood and Society.* New York: W. W. Norton, 1950.

Selma H. Fraiberg. *The Magic Years.* New York: Charles Scribner's Sons, 1959.

Harold D. Gardner. *Frames of Mind.* New York: Basic Books, 1985.

Anita Gurian and Ruth Formanek. *The Socially Competent Child.* Boston: Houghton Mifflin Co., 1983.

Stephen Nowicki, Jr., and Marshall P. Duke. *Helping the Child Who Doesn't Fit In.* Atlanta: Peachtree Press, 1992.

Stanley Turecki, M.D. *The Difficult Child.* New York: Bantam Books, 1985.

D. W. Winnicott. *The Child, The Family and the Outside World.* Boston: Addison-Wesley, 1987.

―――. *Playing and Reality.* New York: Routledge, 1991.

―――. *Talking to Parents.* Boston: Addison-Wesley, 1993.

BOOKS FOR THE YOUNGER CHILD

Lenore Blegvad. *Anna Banana and Me.* New York: Macmillan Child Group, 1987.

Beverly Cleary. *Ellen Tibbets.* New York: Avon Books, 1990.

Lucille Clifton. *Everett Anderson's Friend.* New York: Henry Holt & Co., 1992.

Miriam Cohen. *Best Friends.* New York: Macmillan Child Group, 1989.

―――. *Will I Have a Friend?* New York: Macmillan Child Group, 1989.

Ellen Conford. *Anything for a Friend.* New York: Bantam Books, 1992.

Eloise Greenfield. *Big Friend, Little Friend.* New York: Writers & Readers Publishing, 1991.

P. K. Hallinan. *That's What a Friend Is.* Nashville, Tenn.: Ideals Publishing Corp. 1985.

Helme Heine. *Friends.* New York: Macmillan Child Group, 1982.

Kevin Henkes. *Chester's Way.* New York: Puffin Books, 1989.

Russell Hoban. *Best Friends for Francis.* New York: Harper & Row, 1969.

Katharine Holabird. *Angelina and Alice*. New York: Clarkson Potter, 1987.

Pat Hutchins. *My Best Friend*. New York: Greenwillow Books, 1993.

Arnold Lobel. *Frog and Toad Are Friends*. New York: HarperCollins Child Books, 1985.

Russo Marisabina. *Alex Is My Friend*. New York: Greenwillow Books, 1992.

Else H. Minarik. *Little Bear's Friend*. New York: HarperCollins Children's Books, 1985.

Muriel Pepin. *Little Bear's New Friend*. New York: Reader's Digest Assoc., 1992.

Fred Rogers. *Making Friends*. New York: G. P. Putnam's Sons, 1987.

Anna Ross. *Be My Friend*. New York: Random House, 1991.

Elizabeth-Ann Sachs. *A Special Kind of Friend*. New York: Macmillan Children's Book Group, 1991.

Carol P. Saul. *Peter's Song*. New York: Simon & Schuster, 1992.

William Steig. *Amos and Boris*. New York: Puffin Books, 1977.

Yoriko Tsutsui. *Anna's Best Friend*. New York: Puffin Books, 1989.

BOOKS FOR THE OLDER CHILD (SEVEN AND UP)

Judy Blume. *Iggie's House*. New York: Dell Publishing Co., 1970.

Betsy Byars. *The Pinballs*. New York: Harper Trophy, 1977.

Rosa Guy. *Friends*. New York: Bantam Books, 1981.

Kevin Henkes. *Words of Stone*. New York: Greenwillow Books, 1992.

Myron Levoy. *Alan and Naomi*. New York: HarperCollins Child Books, 1987.

Katherine Paterson. *Bridge to Tarabithia*. New York: HarperCollins Child Books, 1987.

Louis Sacher. *There's a Boy in the Girls' Bathroom*. New York: Knopf Books for Young Readers, 1987.

Marilyn Singer. *Twenty Ways to Lose Your Best Friend.* New York: HarperCollins, 1990.

Mary Stolz. *The Bully of Barkham Street.* New York: HarperCollins Child Books, 1985.